The Church in Crises

The Church in Crises

Kenneth G Morris

Empowered Publications Inc.
Leroy, Alabama
www.empoweredpublicationsinc.com

Photo credit to Lena K's Photography.

Cover Design by Christian Author Partners.

Published by Empowered Publications Inc.
26812 Highway 43
Leroy, Alabama 36548

LCCN:

ISBN: 978-0-9909542-2-4

Table of Contents

INTRODUCTION

Love for the church is deeply embedded in my heart, and it is only right that it should be so. My entire life has been lived with the church as its nucleus. My father was pastoring a church in the state of Alabama at the time of my birth. My years of childhood and youth were spent growing up in parsonages which were located next door to the churches my father pastored. At one time, we actually lived in the church building itself. At the age of eighteen, I entered into the ministry. For the past twenty-five years, I have been engaged in pastoring, and preaching revivals, and campmeetings.

It stirs something within me when I see the spiritual condition that exists in the church today, especially when I think back on what I have known the church to be.

This book is a result of that stirring. It is with no ill will, spite, or animosity toward any one person or any group of people that I have written this book.

The purpose of this book, and my prayer to God for it, is that it might play a part in helping to bring revival to this generation. If this can be so, then the many hours of labor that have gone into it will not have been in vain.

I ask that it be read with an open mind and a prayerful attitude, allowing the spirit to stir your heart.

Sincerely,
Kenneth G. Morris

Chapter One
THE DECLINE AND RISE AGAIN OF THE CHURCH

AND SAMSON CALLED UNTO THE LORD, AND
SAID, O LORD GOD, REMEMBER ME, I PRAY THEE,
AND STRENGTHEN ME, I PRAY THEE, ONLY THIS
ONCE, O GOD, THAT I MAY BE AT ONCE AVENGED
OF THE PHILISTINES FOR MY TWO EYES.
~ JUDGES 16:28

The prayer that Samson prayed in his closing hour on this earth, should be on the lips of every Christian alive today. "O Lord God remember me, I pray thee, only this once, that I may be at once avenged of the Philistines for my two eyes. In the closing hours of the church, O God, let us see Your glory and power one more time."

The question on my mind and heart is; **Will God restore His church before the coming of the Lord?**

Is it not true to say, we are a far cry from where we should be, have been, and ought to be today? We give thanks to God for those among us who are holding on to God, and are maintaining a right position before Him. Let these be encouraged to continue to hold on.

The disturbing thing to my mind, and the minds of countless others, is:

- Where is the power of God that belongs to the

church, and should be operating in the church?
- Where is the glory of God?
- Where are the signs, wonders, and miracles of God?
- What is causing the decline of the church?
- Will the church be restored to its place?

These are important questions. Let's consider them prayerfully with an open mind. It may be, that if we will allow ourselves to see the truth of these things, and not allow Satan to blind us to this truth, "The truth will set us free."

Samson is an Old Testament picture of this very thing. Maybe, we can establish a parallel between the church and Samson. If we discover what caused Samson's decline, maybe, we can see our own shortcomings. If we learn how Samson gained restoration, then perhaps, we can also achieve restoration in our church today.

It is my sincere hope that it will happen, for without a revival of restoration, we will lose a generation to this world, and to the evils of this world.

The coming of the Lord is upon us. Soon there will be the sounding of a trumpet, the shout of the Archangel will be heard, and the dead in Christ will arise from their graves.

I think it is time for us to realize what type of church Christ is coming back after. He is not coming after a dead church. He is not coming after a cold, lukewarm, weak church. He is coming after a virgin whose lamp is filled with oil, with that lamp's wick properly trimmed, and that lamp burning brightly. The foolish virgin that has lost the oil will be shut outside.

When Christ returns for His bride—the church—will He not be looking for the same things that He left when He ascended to the Father? He left a powerful church. Will He return for a weak church? He left a pure church. Will He return for a polluted church? He left a praying church. Will He return for a playing church? He left a giving church. Will He return for a selfish and greedy church? He left a church casting out devils. Will He return for a church that has given Satan a seat, made him comfortable, and welcomed in our midst?

Too many churches are in the devil petting business today. He pays good money into our treasury, and brings prestige to our church, so we feel we must see that he is happy to be sure we keep him.

Is the church—as we know it now—ready for the rapture? If we answer this all important question in light of scripture, then I don't see that the church has adorned herself as a bride—a bride that has made herself ready for the wedding.

This very fact causes me to want to cry out with a fervent cry to God for mercy. Christian men and women of this hour must cry out fervently and without delay! If we fail to pray now, then "All hope that we should be saved will be taken away."

There are those individuals and groups who can say, "I am ready for the rapture." Thank God for these, but where is the church "That's about the Masters business?" The Word of God declares that to those who enter into Heaven the father will say, "well done." What have we "well done?" This is the question we must deal with now. Have we *done well*, in the task of leading believers on to the fullness of the Pentecostal experience? Have we *done well* in our ministry to the sick and suffering?

Our fund raising has done well. Our building programs have done well. Our athletic departments have done very well. Our entertainment has done well, but do these really count? I think not.

To be ready for the rapture, we must do the work of the church well. We must be about the Father's business. For this to be done in this evil day, we need—in deed we must have—an old time revival with a fresh outpouring of the Holy Ghost, and a new and fresh baptism of fire.

Without this revival that I speak of, many churches would be affected very little if the rapture should take place. Perhaps all some churches would lose would be the Nursery Class. Other than that things might remain normal for them.

One minister estimated that fifteen percent of church folk are at this present time ready for the rapture. If we go by the guidelines of some liberal theological groups that have appointed themselves to be some kind of authority, then there might seem to be a greater percentage ready. If we judge this by the Word of God, we must fear that *there be few that find it.* Many today can recall when this was not so.

Many remember a church about the Masters business. A church doing well in the matters of soul salvation, Holy Ghost baptisms, and divine healing. A strange situation exist in the church world today. One group holds onto a particular teaching or truth while letting go completely of other truths that are just as biblical as the one they hold so dear. Another group just a mile or so down the road will treasure the very truth that the first group esteems so low. The first group may hold to the doctrine of speaking in tongues, and at the same time forsake the doctrine of holiness and separation from that which is evil. Another group will cling to the doctrine of holiness with a death grip, while abandoning the truth of divine healing by the power of God through faith in the name of Jesus. There are many other examples, I am sure, to which we could refer.

These situations prevail among us because as the church declines, and finds itself out of touch with the power of God and the manifestations of that power, then we must have some factor to identify with, and that will become our identity before men. We should not be known as a people that embrace one certain principle, but rather be a people identified by the fact that we are in touch with the very power of heaven!

We will know—and the people around us will know—that we are what God wants us to be when we *do the works that Christ did.*

Are we supposed to do the works of Christ? Jesus himself said that not only would we do the works that He did, but greater! We are to *equal* and *surpass* the works of Christ. If this is what the church should be doing, then my dear friends, we are certainly in a state of decline.

Having been in church all of my life, being the son a preacher, I have witnessed the declining trend of God's people. There are many alive today who have watched as the body of Christ, has gone from *power house* for God to *society meeting house* without God. Nothing can take from me the memory of those days. The lost were saved. They did not just make a profession of faith, they were converted. They were changed. Being made new creatures in Christ Jesus, they became brand new! Men and women were baptized in the Holy Ghost. Not just a *prayer language*, but a real baptism. A baptism so real, some had to be carried away from the meeting place, unable to stand or walk. Totally unaware of their physical surroundings. Some were unable to speak in their own tongue until sometime later.

One young lady, with whom I was acquainted, was filled with the spirit in such a manner. Carried home from the service about midnight, she did not speak in her natural tongue before going to bed and to sleep. The next morning, an uncle—a minister who did not believe in this sort of thing—came to speak with her about the happenings of the night before. This uncle asked her to tell him and to describe to him to the best of her ability, exactly what had happened. Attempting to tell him of her experience, as she opened her mouth to speak, the spirit began to speak through her in an unknown tongue. Needless to say, the preacher uncle was astounded, not knowing what to say.

In the church of my early years, miracles of healing and deliverance were wrought at the hands of those who had committed themselves wholly to God and His work.

In this generation, we have advanced in the world—advanced materially—but what has all this profited us? While gaining the world, may God help us to see what we have lost. As our eyes are opened, and we see the things that have slipped from us, may there be a cry coming from our broken hearts that will *Rend Heaven*. A cry for revival and restoration.

We have prayed, but have we prayed for what God wanted, or have we prayed from a heart of pride and greed? We have asked God to fill the church, but maybe God is more interested in purifying the church than in filling it.

Our prayer in this crucial hour, must be a prayer for cleansing.

A prayer for purging. A prayer for renewing. New wine must never be put in old bottles.

We must allow God to put us in His wash pot, put a fire under us, and cleanse us. We must—through our deeds and actions—cleanse ourselves.

What—oh what—will it take to show us this need of cleansing and of sanctification?

For King David, as he and the people of Israel attempted to move the Ark of God, in a manner that was displeasing to God, a man died. This death caused David to seek and find God's way of moving the Ark. It is a sad thing when calamity must come before we will seek God. What will it take?

Now let us consider Samson's decline and restoration. Samson was to Israel what the church is to the world today. He was their one and only hope of deliverance. Does the world of today have any hope outside the church and Christian community?

The call of God had set Samson apart from the rest of humanity. A holy standard of living was placed on him by the word of God. This standard identified him as God's instrument of deliverance for Israel. The Philistine rule and bondage over Israel could now be broken. God had raised Him up a man. It was obvious that Samson was different from others around him.

Samson must never cut his hair, nor partake of the fruit of the vine in any state. He could not eat the grapes, fresh or dried, neither could he drink grape juice.

These were *rules* that Samson must live by. Only by obeying these rules, would the power of God operate in his life.

Is this not a true picture of the church? Is not the church the only hope for these times? Have not we been called of God and set apart by a holy standard? That standard being the word of God, the Bible. Do we not have a commandment to "Come out of the world and touch not the unclean thing?"

When will we learn an all important lesson? To have the power of God, and to see that power manifested in our lives, we *must* live by God's rules.

- To obey is better than sacrifice.
- Rebellion is as the sin of witchcraft.

To break the rule is to lose!

If this sounds like strange sayings to your ears, dear reader, then perhaps you should have a conversation with Adam. Ask Adam if a person can break the rules, and yet live in Eden and enjoy the blessings of God.

If Adam's experience is not convincing enough, then maybe you should visit with King Saul on the last night of his life when disobedience to God's commands had robbed him of God's presence. In this terrible state, he goes to a witch in Endor. The next day he falls on his own sword, in an attempt to commit suicide.

Still not convinced? Then speak with the prophet Jonah. Surely, his three day experience in the whale's belly will be enough to convince you.

If Samson cannot live with the rules God has placed on him, then he cannot be Samson. If the church cannot live with the rules God has placed on her, then she cannot be the church.

First, Samson's eye was always looking in the direction of the Philistines—the world. The Philistine women are appealing to him, always. The women of Israel have NO appeal to him. His desires and emotions were all touched by forbidden things. It seems all his pleasure and thrills come from the ungodly. These are sure steps on the road to ruin.

It is a shameful thing when Christ and Christ-like things do not satisfy the ones who profess Christ. When the church turns itself toward the world and worldly things for pleasure and satisfaction, we can be sure that spiritual things will suffer greatly.

In Judges Chapter fourteen, Samson found a woman of Timnath. The Bible says this thing was from the Lord. This statement may be confusing to some so I will attempt to explain it. God gave Samson *favor* with this Philistine woman, that he might gain an advantage over the Philistines. However, Samson allowed his flesh to become involved and fell in love with her. Instead of Samson gaining an advantage over the Philistines through this relationship, the Philistines were able to manipulate Samson.

We can illustrate this with a picture from religion today. God many times has given his church *favor* with the world so that our message might get through to them. Instead of using this *favor* to expand the gospel, too many times we have fallen in love with the things that God only wanted us to have *favor* with.

Samson, after letting flesh get control proclaimed, "She pleaseth me well." What a statement to make about the enemy!

Now, he will marry the enemy! How sad. The thing that would love to see Samson dead will now become his companion.

- How can we expect victory when the enemy is our companion?
- Can we overcome forces of evil?
- Is this the way to victory?
- Or is this the road to decline?
- Can we remain as we are and maintain what we have if we wed the foe?

The answer to all of these questions is NO! NO! In the strongest use of the word.

There is absolutely no way Samson can expect to continue to be successful in his fight against the Philistines after he makes one of them his companion.

The church, like Samson, is in decline when we join forces with the world. Whether it pleases us to hear it or not, the truth is, the church has married the world.

The holy things of God have ceased to please us. The power of God does not satisfy us. Spiritual things are not enough so we have turned and are continuing to turn to the world and the things of the world to please us and give us a feeling of contentment.

There is a misconception among us that unless we give a certain worldly enticement to draw people to our services, then they will not come. To me, we are confused when we use worldly things to draw people to church, so we can preach to them, and teach them to "LOVE NOT THE WORLD NEITHER THE THINGS THAT ARE IN THE WORLD."

How can Samson destroy the one he has married? How can the church preach and teach against the things used to get people into church? That which was once the enemy of the church has now become the companion of the church.

We have paid a price, a dear price for this union. We have paid with the lives and souls of a generation that has never seen the church be the church—pure and simple.

Generations past believed the Holy Ghost could do His work without any help from this world. They felt the power of God was *all sufficient*. By their actions, many today seem to suggest that God needs help!

Who is right?

- The generations who believed God was able?
- Or this generation who portray a weak or invalid God?
- Can the Holy Ghost build his church without the help of this world and worldly things?
- Can the spirit of God no longer draw a man?
- Do we now have to draw him with the entertainment of this world?

Now a very important question must be raised. If the spirit of God, through some weakness and lack of strength, is unable to draw a man, will this weakened spirit be able to save him? If we use carnal things to *help the Spirit draw him* what will we use to *help the Spirit save him*?

Dear reader, this is a gross insult to the spirit of God. The spirit of God is "well able" to do the work of spiritual things. The Holy Ghost does not need Hollywood or Nashville.

The Holy Ghost only needs those who will submit to Him wholly. The spirit of God needs only a clean, pure, and sanctified church in which to work. Let us give God these simple things and we will witness a great revival with a mighty outpouring of the Holy Ghost.

External things may bring a crowd but they will not bring a soul cleansing revival. We cannot "cast out Beelzebub with

Beelzebub."

Christ in His earthly ministry did not need the Pharisees, Publicans, the Chief Priest, or any others. All He needed was the Holy Ghost which His Father had anointed Him with. The dove that lit on Jesus when John baptized Him in Jordan was enough. Enough to cleanse the leper, enough to feed the multitudes, enough to walk on water, calm the storms, and raise the dead. It was enough to ascend to the Father when His work on Earth was finished. The church is the body of Christ.

The church is the bride of Christ. The church belongs to Christ, therefore we need not this world or its gimmicks. All we need to empower us to *go about doing good* is the same thing that empowered Christ—The Holy Ghost.

Loving the world leads to further temptations. As Samson was going to see the thing that *pleased him*, he came to the vineyards of Timnath, and no doubt passed through them.

Samson's vow to be a Nazarite forbids the consumption of grapes in any form. Why should he subject himself to temptation by passing through the vineyards? It is a dangerous thing to pass through the vineyard when we have a conviction against eating grapes. This generation has witnessed spiritual decline as we have allowed ourselves to pass through the vineyards of forbidden fruit.

Let us consider the possible reasons Samson might have passed through this arena of forbidden fruit. First of all he was headed in a direction he should not have been headed in. Or at least he was going this way for the wrong reason. He should go toward Timnath only as a servant of God to do the work and will of God. Not for carnal pleasure.

The church today should stop and check our spiritual compass. Which direction are we headed, and are we going that way for the right reasons.

In the book of Genesis, Lot traveled toward Sodom, not as a minister, but to enjoy the pleasure of Sodom. Abraham also looked toward Sodom, but his interest was the salvation of the souls that were about to be destroyed there.

The church must look toward this world only with a burden to rescue perishing souls that are trapped in it. Not to partake of its sins.

Secondly, the path through the vineyard could have been a short cut. A time saver. A convenience.

Oh. the short cuts we have found.

- A short cut to prayer. No more crying before God, no more interceding, no more agonizing with God. Just confess it.
- A short cut to preaching. Fasting and praying for a message from God is out of style with our modern day preacher boys. A quick trip to the bookstore is much easier and convenient. No more searching the scriptures. Just a sermon book published by a man far removed from our situation and location.
- A short cut to the Baptism in the Holy Ghost for believers. No more seeking. No more tarrying. It is so easy now, just repeat some sound, imitating some human being.

Then no doubt, he walked through the vineyard to enjoy the comforting shade it provided for his *flesh*. Even though Samson is forbidden from eating the fruit of the vineyard, he allows his flesh to be pampered by the shade of the vineyard.

See this picture. Many have convictions against such things as lying, cheating, stealing, adultery, incest, homosexuality, and murder. They would not think of becoming involved in such things, yet they allow themselves to be entertained and pleased by these things. Many take great pleasure in watching things on television that they would never allow themselves to do. Songs which sing of a lifestyle we do not permit, books which tell of ungodly things give far too many church folk an exceeding amount of pleasure.

My friend beware! It is dangerous to "Pass through the vineyard!" It is hard to continually take pleasure in something, and yet keep ourselves separated from that thing. "Lead us not into temptation, but deliver us from evil." There must have been a reason Christ taught us to pray this prayer.

Next, Samson's declining path took him to Gaza. There the enemy attempted to capture him by closing the gates.

- Many churches are bound.
- Many Christians are bound.
- Many preachers are bound.

This bondage—many times—is a result of being where we should not be, and indulging in things we should not be indulging in.

Samson only went to Gaza for a brief visit. He did not intend to spend the night there. But arising, he found the gate locked.

Did the church ever intend to become so worldly? Did we ever intend to become locked in with the world? This bondage, which perhaps we never planned nor intended, has contributed to the declining trend of the church.

Samson continues in this downward path as he visits and falls in love with another Philistine girl. It seems that by now he would have learned. Like Samson, it seems the church continues to lust after the things of this world.

Samson had his *friend* in Timnath, and was deceived by her. He had his *friend* in Gaza and escaped only through the mercy and power of God. Now having failed to learn a lesson, he finds another *friend*. He finds Delilah.

God, in His mercy, has brought him through many things in spite of a spirit of worldly lust. Could it be that Samson believes that just because of who he is, God will not turn away and take his power from him? If this is true, then this man is about to learn a great lesson. He is going to learn, "My spirit does not always strive with man."

My soul trembles, as I see the church take the same course of action, and be possessed by the same mentality as Samson. As surely as we have flirted with the world, we have met our Delilahs, who through a false face of friendship, have robbed us of too much of the power of God.

Samson lays his head in Delilah's lap. He has a vow on that

head. A Nazarite must never cut his hair. If he is not to cut his hair, then he never should've allow the enemy to play with his head.

Satan is playing with a lot of Christian's heads.

- Toying with their convictions.
- Tampering with their standard of holiness.
- Persuading them that God will not hold them responsible.

Delilah played on Samson's emotions. "If you love me," was her favorite line. This is a thing of passion. An affair with the world—a relationship with sin—will do to one what one never intended it to do.

Do you think Samson went to Delilah's house with the intentions of losing his power? Certainly, he did not. A hair cut was not in his plans. But it happened! It happened!

When the church began its impassioned relationship with this world;

- Did we intend to lose the things we had?
- Did we intend to lose the power to convict sinners of sin?
- Did we intend to rob ourselves of a true Pentecostal blessing?
- Did we intend to stop healing the sick and relieving the suffering?

No! A million times no! But, my dear friend, look around you, it has happened! The evidence and proof is overwhelming. It has happened.

Consider these things:

- Marrying the enemy,
- Being pleased by forbidden things,
- Passing through the vineyards of temptations,
- Walking in forbidden territory,
- Allowing the enemy to tamper with standards and convictions.

It is no small wonder that Samson lost his power, and was reduced to the ranks of normal men. His strength is now no more than any other man.

What a shame!

The church has followed the same path, and has been reduced to a mere social gathering. We operate in only the natural realm, where once we operated in the supernatural. We once healed our sick. We settled our differences at the altar. Things have changed.

Samson was restored. This restoration was a dreadful and a painful thing. We want Christ to restore the church today, but we want Him to do it pleasantly and painlessly. Not so my friend. Restoration to our former place will of necessity be a painful process.

It was painful to Samson to have his eyes burned from their sockets with hot, iron rods. The vision that had so often led him astray had to be taken away. If he is restored with his sight, it will only be a matter of time before he lusts again.

It is a painful remedy, but a necessary one.

Much of the "vision" that led the church of this generation down was religious television. We thank God for all he has done and for all the methods he has used, but we must be very candid and honest with ourselves. Many today would be living still by the standards of old time religion if they had not been exposed to so-called religious television. We had convictions against a worldly appearance, a flesh glorifying expression, and entertainment that bordered on worldliness. But we saw it on religious television, and lo and behold, it was shedding tears. It was weeping and rejoicing. And wonders of wonders, it was speaking in tongues.

Could it be that the collapse of much of religious television programming, and especially the Pentecostal variety, is God's first step in the restoration of His church? Is this the burning out of the eyes?

When Samson could no longer see his temptations, then he could see himself in his pitiful condition. He could now see what he had lost.

With the glamour gone, with the fleshly sparkle gone, with mega bucks religion no longer before our eyes, it just might be that we will see ourselves as we are "Poor, blind, and naked." It might be that we will remember "The glory of the former house," and cry out to God to send His glory to this "latter house."

Now that we may not be able to see our favorite preacher and his entertainment, maybe we will see Christ and His glory.

Feel the torture as the Philistines bind the hands that have for so long enjoyed a powerful dominance and freedom. Hands that have enjoyed so much power and freedom, now are bound. These hands had been free, but in their liberty they were allowed to touch forbidden things. For restoration to come, this liberty had to be severely restricted.

In America, we have enjoyed freedom and liberty in our worship. Will God use some legislative restrictions, coming out of Washington and our state capitols to *bind our hands*? Will it take this sort of thing to get us to pray through? Restrictions on our religious liberty may cause us to recognize our need for God. When we are told what we can and cannot preach, then we will cry "O Lord God, Remember me." When laws are passed that forbid us to cry out against the great sins of our day; abortion, homosexuality, etc., then a prayer meeting announcement will appear on many church bulletins. If we are told by government, and don't think it cannot happen, that we cannot exclude from membership in our church any who desire to join it, regardless of their lifestyle, then "weeping will be heard in Zion." Restoration will be painful.

Thirdly, Samson was forced to grind at the mill. Oh, how humiliating that must have been! Restoration is not only painful, it is humiliating! Humility is a vital part of restoration.

- His vision is gone.
- He's bound and restricted.
- He's grinding at the mill.

When churches are forced to *grind at the mill*, forced to pay taxes to the state and national government to help pay for federally funded abortion, and other such things, the cry for help will be heard. When after paying these taxes, we cannot pay the mortgage on our extravagant real estate, the pastor's salary has to be reduced, athletics have to be discontinued, and we can no longer afford the world's entertainment, the church will pray, **"O LORD GOD, REMEMBER ME, I PRAY THEE, AND STRENGTHEN ME, I PRAY THEE, ONLY THIS ONCE."**

Chapter Two
CHRISTIANS IN ADVERSITY

YEA, AND ALL THAT WILL LIVE GODLY IN
CHRIST JESUS SHALL SUFFER PERSECUTION.
BUT EVIL MEN AND SEDUCERS SHALL WAX
WORSE AND WORSE, DECEIVING, AND
BEING DECEIVED. BUT CONTINUE THOU IN
THE THINGS WHICH THOU HAST LEARNED,
AND HAST BEEN ASSURED OF, KNOWING OF
WHOM THOU HAST LEARNED THEM.
~ II TIMOTHY 3:12- 4

The declining nature of the church, and the degenerating condition of the world puts the true Christian of this age in a peculiar position. We are living in one of the most adverse times that Christians have ever known.

How can these times compare to the persecution of the early church, some might ask? This is a legitimate question and the answer is quite simple. In the persecution of the first century, the political, religious, and social communities rejected Christ and all His teachings. Not only did they reject the Beatitudes, they rejected the one who preached the Sermon on the Mount. They not only refused to acknowledge His works, they denied that He was the Christ.

The adversary today has taken an approach that is vastly

different. To a large extent, the political, religious, and social communities now accept Jesus. They agree to the fact of His life, death and resurrection. Many accept His virgin birth. Yet, while professing a belief in the historical Christ, they do not accept His doctrine and teaching.

So which is the greater evil? For the Christian, which becomes the greater threat?

In the first century an acknowledgment of Christ was enough to bring punishment and death on many occasions. There was a clear, precise line drawn. There could be no doubt where one stood. No gray, fuzzy, neutral zone existed. Either you were, or you were not. The individual and everyone around him knew what he was and where he stood. It was hot or cold. No lukewarmness existed.

In the late twentieth century one can express a *belief in Christ* and be accepted. Some have even become national leaders and heroic symbols while proclaiming their faith. Yet, at the same time to profess a *belief in the doctrines and teachings of Christ* makes one unacceptable and politically incorrect.

As we compare the first century persecution with the late twentieth century adversity, the question to be answered is a simple one. In which era would it be easier to please God? Of course it is much easier to profess a belief in Christ now than then. Many exercise a beautiful lip service to Him, but Jesus said, "Not everyone that sayeth to me Lord, Lord, shall enter into the kingdom of Heaven; but he that doeth the will of my Father which is in Heaven."

From which circumstance would it be easier to go to Heaven? This is an age of deception and seduction. Many men and women are deceived into thinking that to profess Christ is all that is necessary for salvation. This is a trick of the adversary. We cannot embrace Christ's person, and at the same time reject what he stands for. Can we love the one who died on a cross to remove sin and at the same time promote sin, and sinful things? Friend, do not forget the words of Christ, "If you love me keep my commandments."

The line between the Christian and the unsaved is not as clear as it once was. There is a danger of being seduced into believing a lie and being lost. Believing ourselves to be saved by a religious formality, and forgetting that *a tree is known by its fruit.*

As Christians we must keep our guard up at all times. God expects no less out of this generation than He has any previous generation. We cannot excuse ourselves in our lack of commitment, obedience, and service to God by saying that the church is in decline. We must not persuade ourselves that this is a new age and things have changed.

Sure things have changed. Things have changed drastically, but God has not changed. Sure the church is in a lukewarm state, yet the desire of Christ for us as individuals is still that we be hot or cold.

Do not excuse yourself dear friend, for Christ will not excuse you on that day when you stand before Him. The *password* into Heaven is still, "Well done thou good and faithful servant."

The great apostle Paul described these days with a true and vivid description in the third chapter of Second Timothy. Hear him as he describes these times as perilous. Men, he said, would be proud, boastful, covetous, blasphemers, unthankful, ungodly, etc. It is true today that men love pleasure and love themselves more than they love God.

Paul also warns of the abortionist and homosexuals that would arise in our day. When he stated that men—and this includes women too—would be without natural affection. It is not natural for a mother to murder her child through an act called abortion. It is not natural for a man or woman to become sexually involved with one of the same sex.

This generation is also described as a people who have a form of godliness, but deny the power thereof. This is a description of the church in decline. We are told by the apostle to turn away from this kind.

Resisting the truth is another identifying characteristic of this age. Resisting the truth has created a generation of humanity with corrupt, reprobate minds concerning the faith.

We of this generation must strive to please God in the midst of all these things. Can it be done? Some are convinced that it cannot. Paul knew that it could be done, so in the twelfth through fourteenth verses of this II Timothy chapter three he has given to us instructions and guidelines for survival in these last days.

We are warned that persecution will come, not to those who profess only, but to those that *Will live Godly in Christ Jesus.* The pressure is being applied to those who will not compromise and accept ungodliness. Following this warning of coming persecution—and a warning that evil men and seducers shall wax worse and worse—we are told to continue in the things we have learned and have been assured of.

Don't forget the old time religion! In verse fifteen Paul admonishes Timothy and us to not forget the things we learned as a child. We are also told by Paul, as he writes in another place to Timothy, that we should have in us the *unfeigned faith* of generations past.

Many have ignored these warnings and instructions, and have been rocked to sleep in the cradle of compromise. This is a dangerous thing. We must not despise these *safety instructions* from our survival manual. It is time to "Awake O sleeper and call on God."

Hell has broken loose on the earth and Satan is attacking everything that is holy and good.

Christian principles are being bombarded on every side. The family and home, morality, and everything that is decent is being scorned and laughed at today. Real Christians are being identified now by the fact that we stand for the standards and truths of past generations. It is not always easy to resist the trend of society.

We were not told it would be easy, but we are told it will be worth it. It **is not** a picnic. It **is** a battlefield. If it was a picnic, then our reward would be indigestion and sunburn. It's a battlefield, and our reward will be victory. A victor's crown! Hold on brother and sister. Fight the fight, keep the faith, and win the crown.

Can this victory be won in the face of adversity? Can this

victory be won when Hell is attacking so violently? Yes, it can be won and it will be won by many. Oh sure, some will fall by the wayside, but many will *keep the faith and finish the course.* Stephen did it. Paul did it. We can do it too.

There's one thing to be sure of—adversity separates the real from the fake. There are many who wear the mask of Christianity. Adversity will remove that mask. Only the real, the genuine, the true will stand.

There's a story in the Old Testament that proves this. It's the story of Daniel in Babylon. Let's consider this story that we may draw strength from it. A man who not only survived, but excelled in adversity. Daniel's circumstance was similar to ours in many ways. We're serving the same God Daniel served. If God's grace was sufficient for Daniel, then His grace is sufficient for us. What was Daniel's secret? How did he do it? These are the things we shall now look into.

Daniel was not influenced by changes in laws and social customs. When this young man and others like him were carried away from Jerusalem as captives to Babylon, they were exposed to many legal and social changes. Living under the laws of Babylon was a great change from living under the laws of Jerusalem. Daniel finds many things now legal and lawful that were a short time ago illegal and unlawful. Not only are these things legal and lawful, they are encouraged.

In Jerusalem it was unlawful to eat bread and drink wine that had been offered in sacrifice to idols. In Babylon it was lawful.

We can draw a distinct parallel here. Many things are legal in the United Stated of America today that only a few years ago were against the law. Before 1973, it was unlawful in America to abort a baby. Now, it is lawful and the law protects actions that were once against the law. For many years, homosexuals were forbidden to serve in our military. Now, that isn't so.

- What is the responsibility of a Daniel in Babylon or a born again Christian in the United States when laws are enacted that contradict the laws of God?

- Is Daniel free to eat the bread and drink the wine of Babylon just because the law of the land says it's legal?
- Does the changes in human laws free him from God's laws?
- If he ate this bread in Jerusalem, he would have been doing wrong, but is it wrong now that he is in Babylon and living under a new set of laws?
- Is it all right now for a Christian to have an abortion? The law of the land has changed.
- Is homosexuality an alternate lifestyle? Should it be accepted by the church and into the church now that governments have changed, and are now accepting them?

NO, dear friend, NO. Washington may change the law of the land, but Washington D. C. will never change the law of God.

The law of the land may be altered and changed to the point that sin and sinful things become acceptable in our society. Homosexuality may be accepted as an alternate lifestyle in our communities, but the real Christian and the true church can never accept this into our lives and churches.

Abortion has been legalized. It's a woman's choice they say, but what does God say? God says, "Thou shalt not kill." Is abortion murder?

At what point does life begin?

For Jeremiah the prophet, life began in his mother's womb. I don't think God would call someone to be a prophet before he begins to live, and the Bible tells us plainly that Jeremiah was called to be a prophet from his mother's womb, while he was yet unborn.

Could or would God fill a dead, nonliving something with the Holy Ghost? I don't think so. Well, John the Baptist was filled with the Holy Ghost in his mother Elizabeth's womb as she heard Mary tell how she had been chosen to become the mother of the Messiah.

Let laws be passed and court rulings be handed down to try

to determine when life begins. Let them tell us at what point a fetus becomes a living person. The church and the children of God already know the answers to these questions. From God's word, we know that life begins with conception. So we cannot and will not change our thoughts, because we are governed by the unchanging word of the Lord.

That God's law is an unchanging law is illustrated very well in the story of Moses and the Ten Commandments. The Ten Commandments were the commandments of God. They were not the commandments of Moses. Moses was not the one who said, "Thou shalt not kill." Therefore, since he was not the author of these commandments, he had no right, nor power to change them. The law had to be delivered to the children of Israel just as it was written by God.

When God recorded the Ten Commandments, He did not have an angel write them for Him, but He wrote them with His own finger. This truth lets us know that there could be no error or mistake in the commandments. No one could say that God intended the commandments to say something else, or to mean something else. He wrote them with His own finger. He did not tell Moses what to write and then let him write it. He wrote it Himself.

It is also important to notice the material on which God wrote His law. The law of God was not written on parchment or paper or any such thing. Friend, this document was not actually written at all. It was engraved in stone. This gives to us a clear message that God's law could not be changed. If this law had been written on parchment or paper, Moses or anyone else could have erased parts and rewrote them to suit themselves or others. Moses could have "taken from or added to." But not so with stone.

Today, some live as if the commandments were written in the sand—changing with every rain or wind of doctrine. If you are numbered among this crowd, be warned, you have believed a lie. The Ten Commandments were not written in the shifting sands of time, but in the Solid Rock.

We know who the Solid Rock is. We know His name. He is the Rock that followed Israel through the wilderness. Jesus Christ is the Solid Rock. The Rock never changes. Hear the scripture say, "Jesus Christ the same yesterday, and today, and forever!" If the stone never changes, then we can be certain that the word written in stone never changes. It is forever settled in Heaven.

As Moses was on the mountain with God receiving the Ten Commandments, strange things were happening in the valley below. The congregation of Israel, believing something has happened to their leader, and that he will not return to them, built an idol in the form of a golden calf, and begin to worship it. The worshipping of the golden calf—no doubt—started out simple enough, but as this ungodliness progressed, it took on a more radical and bizarre atmosphere. The people stripped off their clothes, and danced naked around this so called god which they had made.

It isn't hard for me to imagine the many sins that were taking place in such surroundings. There must have been covetousness, lying, adultery, stealing, murder, and many more forms of evil going on as approximately three million people danced naked around a golden calf.

As all this evil was in full force in the valley, God had finished giving His law to Moses, and it was time for Moses to come down from the mountain and present this law to the congregation.

Coming down a sufficient distance close enough to hear and realize what was happening, we can only imagine the thoughts and feelings of Moses's heart. As he looked upon the people in their nakedness, reveling in iniquity, bold in ungodliness, he was keenly aware of what he held in his hand. Perhaps he would look into the camp, and then look at the commandments in his hand. The question on his mind must have been something like this; How can I carry this law into a situation where most, if not all, the commandments contained in it are being violated at this very moment? What a spot to be in.

How many ministers of the gospel are facing this same situation? How can I bring a message in a situation where the message is being violated?

How many Christian men and women are facing this common problem? How can I carry my Godly convictions and holy standards into a work place where these convictions and standards are mocked and made light of?

- What is Moses to do?
- What is the minister to do?
- What is the Christian to do?
- Can we change the message to fit the crowd?
- Can we change our convictions to more acceptable ones?

It is obvious that Moses cannot change the law and commandments. They are engraved in stone. They do not fit the crowd or the occasion, so what are his options?

There are only two options for Moses to choose from. He can go into the camp with the tables of stone and bring reproach on the children of Israel, or he can cast the tablets to the ground breaking them to pieces. Moses chose the latter and threw the stone tablets to the ground breaking them to pieces.

This is a great lesson for us in our generation. We can either keep the commandments of God, or else we can break them. We cannot change them.

May we catch a glimpse of this scene. The law of God, written by God's own hand, lies on the ground broken to bits. There the pieces lie at Moses's feet on the mountain side. What a sad sight.

This same sad sight exists in many individual Christian lives today. These are defeated Christians. Defeated by Satan as the commandments of God lie broken at their feet. Many homes and churches are overrun by the evil forces of hell as the law of God lies broken before us.

When the unchanging word of God is in contact with the souls of men that are not willing to change and conform to that word, the results are broken commandments and ruined lives.

Moses—after breaking the tablets—is commanded by God to hew another set of tablets from stone, and return to the mountain top to renew the commandments. God will rewrite the law. Did Moses think perhaps God, after having seen the sight in the valley below, would alter the law to make it more pleasing to the actions and desires of the people? Since adultery was being committed in the camp would God leave that part out? Since lust was rampant among that naked, indecent crowd, would He leave out, "Thou shalt not covet thy neighbor's wife?"

If there was any doubt or question in Moses's mind, they soon disappeared as the finger of God began to rewrite the Ten Commandments. For wonder of wonders, He wrote the same thing that He had written before.

After three days in the whale's belly, Jonah also learned the lesson of the unchanging word. "The word of the Lord came unto Jonah the second time saying, "arise, go to Nineveh.""

If we as individual Christians, churches, and homes, intend to survive these days of adversity, we must also learn this lesson. We must pick up the pieces of the broken law of God, put that law together again in our hearts, obey it, and live by it no matter what the cost or consequences.

As we go back to the story of Daniel in Babylon, it does not take long to realize that Daniel had no intentions of breaking the Law of God. As our text has stated, he continues, "In the things he has learned." He is not looking to change or rearrange anything. Although surroundings, circumstances, laws, and customs have changed, he will *continue in the things he has learned.*

To do any different would bring defilement to his heart. Daniel knew one thing for sure; a defiled heart surely would not make it. He knew if he had any hope of surviving this day of adversity, he must keep himself pure. He refuses to compromise the purity of his heart by accepting legalized sin. This legalized sin being bread and wine from the kings table.

There probably were those around who reminded Daniel of the legality of eating this bread and drinking this wine. Things are different now they would say. This is Babylon. This is a new day.

Daniel would accept none of this reasoning. He wanted to

survive. He wanted to make it through. When the end of this captivity came he wanted to be ready for deliverance.

Daniel purposed in his heart not to defile himself. He made a very important decision. A decision that would determine the outcome of his life. Even though he lived in Babylon and was surrounded by Babylonian laws and customs, Daniel would order his life after the laws of Jerusalem.

Even though we live in this world, we must pattern our lives after the laws of Heaven. We hear the terms legality and constitutionality, and political correctness? Is it legal? Is it constitutional? Is it politically correct? These are the guiding principles of the civic minded, but they cannot be the guidelines for the spiritual minded.

- The spiritual minded person does not only ask is it legal, that person also considers whether or not it is right.
- The child of God not only asks if it is constitutional, but also asks is it Biblical.
- The born again Christian is not so much concerned about being politically correct as being spiritually correct in the sight of God.

Daniel was not being politically correct when he informed the eunuch he would not eat the abominable thing. The eunuch was displeased and troubled, but God was pleased and blessed.

It is also politically incorrect in our generation to oppose abortion, and to oppose the lifestyle of the homosexual community. The Supreme Court has decreed abortions constitutional. Gays have rights—our leaders have declared. So, are we out of step with our constitution, and our legal system when we rise up in opposition to these issues? Yes, this position puts us at a difference with the constitution, but it aligns us perfectly with the word of God. We are in opposition to that which is legal, but we ourselves are in full agreement with that which is right.

The constitution is a document that has served us well for a long time. The problem with this document is that the Supreme

Court interprets it for us, and what they say becomes the law of the land.

This is not so with the Bible. Men can say anything they desire about the Bible and what it means, but they will never change it. It is forever settled in Heaven.

Being politically correct and being in agreement with the Supreme Court's interpretation of the constitution will never save us. This stand will not empower us to survive this end time adversity, and be ready when Jesus comes.

The interpretation of the constitution and the laws of the land change with time, but God's word never changes. For instance; before 1973, the constitution, and the laws of the United States would commit to jail those caught in the act of aborting babies. Before 1973, the law of God would condemn the abortionist to hell. Now, the constitution and laws of the land protect those who abort babies. This is a complete turnaround. But the law of God still condemns these to hell.

Up until 1993, the law of the land prohibited gays from serving openly in the military forces of our land. Now, the laws have changed. "Don't Ask, Don't Tell" has been repealed. Gays serve openly in the military, but no matter what the changes in American law may be, gays will never be allowed in Heaven.

Daniel stood firm on his convictions in adversity and would not accept legalized sin. He made it. For us to make it, we must not compromise. We must not accept legalized and constitutionalized sin.

It is not only the federal government that's changing laws. The church governments are also changing their views of right and wrong.

In the thirty-fifth chapter of the book of Jeremiah, there is an interesting story of a group of people. These people are known as the Rechabites. The Rechabites were a people who vowed to never drink wine or strong drink. For many years, they walked passed the taverns and joints of their day, and didn't defiled themselves by breaking their vow. Then God, in an effort to teach a lesson to backslidden Israel, commanded Jeremiah to take wine into the temple. He was then to bring the Rechabites into the temple, and offer to them the wine. This Jeremiah did, but the Rechabites refused to drink even in the temple.

Many people refused certain things as long as the world was offering these things to them, but now the church offers to them the same things and the same activities, and these people accept them and indulge in them.

To spiritually survive these perilous times, we must take an example from the Rechabites and refuse legalized sin even when it is legalized by the church.

Not only did Daniel not allow himself to be influenced by the Babylonian system, he also refused to be intimidated by it. When this man of God refused to defile himself by committing an act of disobedience to God, then the enemies of Daniel tried to intimidate him by restricting his religious liberty. If he will not compromise himself by the sin of commission, it may be that he will sin against God by the sin of omission.

Many today have given in to the pressures of this worldly system that confronts us, and involve themselves in unholy activities that are robbing them of their walk with God. Let these seek a place of repentance quickly, and let them *return to the old landmarks which our fathers have set*, lest He come quickly and *remove the candlestick*.

There are many among us even today that are doing as Daniel did, and are refusing the enticements of this world. Choosing as Moses did "To suffer the reproach of God's people rather than enjoy the pleasures of sin for a season." These maintain their standards and convictions. Their lifestyles reflect a certain holiness of life. Let these be commended and encouraged to *continue in the things they have learned*.

So you—just like Daniel—have stood the test of compromise. But be assured of this one thing; there is surely another test even more severe than this one. You have not been influenced by legalized sin. Now, you must not be intimidated when that which is right is outlawed.

A decree was written and signed with the king's signature which made it illegal to pray to God. This is a true picture of the situation that exists today. Sin is legal. Righteousness is in some cases illegal. While the Supreme Court has decreed that it is legal to murder babies, they have outlawed prayer and Bible reading in schools, and public places. This is unconstitutional they say. While our government gives gays the right to parade themselves and publicly advertise their lifestyle, we are being told not to display religious scenes depicting the birth of Christ on public property at Christmas time.

While the church is offering wine to the Rechabites, so to speak, the church in too many instances is restricting worship even in the sanctuary. To worship with an audible voice in many religious services will get a person very strange looks from the pastor or board of deacons. To say a good, strong, hardy "amen" during a lot of sermons, would cause the minister to lose his place. If you feel the need to pray, there is a designated room down the hall someplace where you can do your praying. It's forbidden in the sanctuary.

We used to tarry around the altar seeking an infilling of the Spirit. That's old fashioned they say. There are no altars to tarry around in most churches today. Churches have their party rooms, but where are the prayer rooms? Our noses guide us to the supper room, but where is the upper room?

If one went into the temples of today "walking and leaping and praising God," as the man did in the third chapter of Acts, an usher would promptly show that one to the door.

So will we be intimidated?

What will we do?

Will we restrict our worship so we can be accepted into the fellowship of some church so long dead that spiritual rigormortis has already set in?

Will we become cold and stiff just so we can sit in a cold congregation, and hear a stiff doctor of theology give some kind of essay on the social sciences of today?

Or will we be like good ole Daniel and say, "I don't care what you say, I'm going to pray anyway?" Knowing the decree had been signed, Daniel, with his window raised toward Jerusalem, prayed three times every day.

Why was Daniel so determined to continue his prayer life and his devotions to God even when it was unlawful? The answer is a simple one. He knew he was living in an environment that could very easily destroy his spiritual life. An environment that would take from him his special touch of God. He did not want this to happen, so in order to survive this day of adversity, Daniel *continued in the things he had learned.*

Let us be sure that his stand was not popular. We will not be popular when we stand for what's right in the day of adversity. When the choice is popularity or salvation, then we must choose salvation.

Daniel is well aware of the consequences of praying. I think we can be reasonably sure that he had visited the vicinity of the lion's den many times. Possibly, he had witnessed lawbreakers being thrown to the lions as penalty for their crimes, and cringed as he watched the lions break the bones and devour the flesh of these criminals. Now, he knows this will be his fate if he continues to pray to the God of Heaven.

Without hesitation or delay, Daniel raised his window and prays. He prayed three times a day before the decree was signed, and he prayed three times a day after the decree has been signed into law.

Far too many today are governed by their surroundings and circumstances. They worship when everyone else worships. They are very bold to ask God's blessings on their meal when in the presence of other Christians, but in the company of unbelievers they are intimidated and refuse to say grace at meal time. When surrounded by spiritually minded people, they are very spiritually minded, but it's a different story when in the presence of carnal thinkers.

These remind me of the lizard that is constantly changing his color to match the color of the leaf or stick he is sitting on. Lizard Christians are what they should be called.

Some will excuse this sort of action by saying they are using wisdom or they are trying to be discrete. We certainly should use wisdom and discretion. However, this is not an excuse for being intimidated. I think some use it so.

Was Daniel being unwise or indiscreet when he continued his devotion to God knowing he would go to the den of lions? Was his action in an ignorant or rash manner? Certainly not. He was indeed being very wise to refuse to allow the system to take from him his fellowship with his master. Likewise, we must stay on our guard so as not to allow the system—both governmental and religious—to cause us to break fellowship with our Lord.

Sure, he is headed for the den of lions. Sure persecutions will come. "As many as live Godly in Christ Jesus shall suffer persecution." He is sure of one thing; he is a child of God and he has kept up his fellowship with God. His God "will never leave him nor forsake him." If Daniel goes to the den of lions, God will also go to the den of lions. It is better to be in the lion's den with God than to be in high society without Him.

Christians today want to have an influence on their friends and loved ones. They feel they must compromise to accomplish this. Daniel has a great influence on the King of Babylon. This influence was so profound that the king made a decree by proclamation that no other god could be worshipped in his kingdom but the God of Daniel. This great prophet made a difference, because he would not be intimidated by the Babylonian system.

The Christian will never make a difference in his or her community by bowing to the pressure of the secular crowd. To make a difference one must be different. It is only as we stand firm in our faith, humbly refusing to bend or bow, that we can make a difference in our own life, and the lives of others around us.

The world is in a sad condition. Salt is desperately needed now. Darkness is fast covering the face of the earth. Light is needed now. Let those who Christ proclaimed to be the *salt of the earth* and *the light of the world* stand and be counted.

We are *Christians in Adversity.* Forces of evil try to influence and intimidate us, but God's grace is sufficient. **BY THAT MARVELOUS GRACE AND THROUGH THE MIGHTY POWER OF GOD, WE SHALL PREVAIL.**

Chapter Three
THIRD CULTURES

AND UNTO THE ANGEL OF THE CHURCH OF
THE LAODICEANS WRITE: THESE THINGS
SAITH THE AMEN, THE FAITHFUL AND TRUE
WITNESS, THE BEGINNING OF THE CREATION
OF GOD: I KNOW THY WORKS, THAT THOU
ART NEITHER COLD NOR HOT. SO THEN
BECAUSE THOU ART LUKEWARM, AND
NEITHER COLD NOR HOT, I WILL SPEW THEE
OUT OF MY MOUTH.

~ REV. 3:14-16

The above scriptures are not the word of the Lord to heathen people that have never heard the teachings of Christianity and Christian principles. This is a message of the spirit to the Laodicean church. The spirit of Christ commanded John to tell a lukewarm church that He would spew them out of His mouth. The lukewarmness of this hour causes a certain sickness to come to the stomach of God Himself. He will vomit it up.

Christ purchased the church with His blood on Calvary. For the church, He suffered, bled, and died. The supreme price was paid. Then, after shedding His blood to purchase the church, Jesus prayed the Father to send another comforter—the Holy Ghost—to empower it. All of this was done in the beginning of the age where we hear this stern warning that the church will be spewed out. This is to say Christ will disown the Laodicean church because of a condition of lukewarmness.

This lets us know that somewhere between the first century of the church, and this present hour something has gone terribly wrong. Someone has made a wrong turn somewhere.

Let us endeavor in this chapter to discover where the church made this wrong turn. What has been the error of the church movement? Where did we "leave our first love?"

In searching for clues to the answers to these questions, let us consider one of the fundamental truths from the Bible concerning our God. Let us consider the fact that God stands for purity. Purity is the standard by which our God operates. All of the laws and statutes are founded on the basics of purity.

One of the very first of God's commandments to his creation was that everything should "bring forth after its own kind." God was never interested in hybrids. "Everything after its kind" was and is the law of God.

The Great Creator's desire at the time of creation was that every one of His creations remain in a pure state even as it was created. No mixing. No mingling. No crossing. No hybrids.

Throughout the many great stories of the Bible, we find that God hated, and refused to accept things that were "mixed up."

To find proof for this statement one must only read the Law of Moses. Read the books of Leviticus, Numbers, and Deuteronomy, and in so doing proof will be found to confirm this truth. Read carefully the twenty second chapter of Deuteronomy and take note of the many calls and demands for purity. Purity is so demanded that the Israelites were forbidden to plant "divers kinds" of seed in the same seed plot.

The blessing of God would not be on a field, if in that field a man was found plowing with an ass and an ox in the same yoke. Even in the clothing and manner of dress there was a call for purity. No garment was to be woven using different kinds of material. The women and the men were forbidden to dress alike and wear the same type of clothing.

In these instructions to the Hebrews, the Almighty is showing His pleasure in things that are pure. He let it be known that He does not want any cross pollinating going on. "Be not unequally yoked together" is a commandment that applies to us today from the New Testament.

When these principles of purity were compromised, God was always displeased. There are many examples from Biblical times that teach this. It will well-serve those of us in this generation who yet desire favor from our God to look carefully at some of these examples.

One of these examples many of us remember from our early Sunday School days is the story of Noah's ark. The flood was stamped into a lot of young minds as we colored our picture cards every Sunday. God destroyed His own creation. The Eternal One was sorry that He made man. What could have happened to cause this?

The Lord was not sorry He made man when Adam and Eve sinned in the garden. He did not repent for creating man after Cain killed his brother Able. But at the time of Noah, He regretted creating man.

Before the time of Adam's sin, Adam was totally pure. He spent all his time in the Garden of Eden. His time was not divided between the garden and the outside world. His was an existence that involved a single culture.

After the fall, Adam was removed from the garden. This removal was total and complete. Even as before when the garden was his one home, now the outside world is his one home. Adam and Eve were not allowed to reenter the garden at all. Never did they go again into the garden.

Even though their fellowship with God is broken and they are out instead of in, they yet live a single culture life.

- They no longer walk with God in the cool of the day.
- They no longer enjoy the benefits of the Garden of Eden.
- They have sinned and transgressed the

commandment of God.
- They have been cast out.

But they have not mixed anything. Therefore God was not sorry that He made them from the dust of the earth.

The first two sons born to Adam and Eve, Cain and Abel, were very different young men. One was righteous, and the other was unrighteous. Cain represented one culture, and Abel represented the other culture. Right—totally right, and wrong—totally wrong are represented by these two boys. God does not regret breathing the breath of life into man's nostrils even after Cain kills his brother Abel, and hides his dead body in the sand. Murder was committed, and murder is a sin. God hates sin, so Cain was punished. He was punished so severely that he felt he would not be able to bear it.

Yet, God did not view humanity as He did in Noah's day. He did not look on mankind with an eye to destroy every living thing that creepeth on the face of the earth. Though Cain's sin was horrible and defied God and everything God stands for, nothing was *mixed*. A new culture is not produced. Unrighteousness destroys righteousness, but a compromise and mixture between the two is not produced.

Now with Abel dead and out of the way, the worldly culture dominates. This situation does not last long however. For after a time, God gave another son to Adam and his wife. This son was called Seth, and he becomes the new head of the righteous culture.

After the birth of Seth the world once again has a two culture system. And even though we can be sure God is not pleased with the unrighteousness of the Cain culture, He has no desire to destroy man from the face of the earth.

We have now seen the express commandment of God broken in the Garden of Eden. We have witnessed the murder of a man by his brother. Both of these sins were dealt with by the Almighty, but no attempt is made to annihilate the human race. Sin has been committed. Wrong has been done, but nothing has been mixed. This may sound like a strange doctrine to some in this age of compromise and mixed up religion, but there can be no disputing the truth of it.

There was no thought of removing man from the face of the earth until the time of Noah. Sure, there was sin and evil on the earth, but we have no record of righteousness mixing with unrighteousness until we come to the sixth chapter of Genesis.

The sixth chapter of the book of Genesis is a crisis chapter. The world had known trouble, sin, and sorrow, but a state of crisis had not existed until this time. Fateful words come from the mouth of God. "My spirit shall not always strive with man."

The word strive means to be in a struggle with, to be in conflict with, or to contend with. Almighty God vowed that He would not always be in conflict with mankind, and would not always struggle with the human race.

This attitude toward man was not seen earlier in any of God's dealing. God threw Adam and Eve out of the garden, but not until He had made them coats or clothing from animal skins. The fig leaves with which they had covered themselves would not last very long or give much protection in the outside world. God knew this, so He replaced their fig leaves with the skins of animals. This speaks plainly to say that even though they had transgressed, God was yet mindful of them.

Did not God show favor to Cain after he killed Abel? After the curse had been pronounced on Cain, and Cain cried in agony and grief of soul that his punishment was greater than he could bear, God responded by proclaiming a sevenfold vengeance on anyone that would slay Cain. Notice carefully that even after so great a sin as murder, God took a definite step to preserve the life of Cain, the murderer.

How can we compare the coats of skin for the transgressors, and the protecting proclamation for the murderer with the decree of judgment for the generation of Noah's day? Are not these that will die in the flood descendants of the ones that were protected from the elements of nature by coats of skin?

God will now destroy the sons and daughters of the murderer that he once preserved from death. The fathers of the age enjoyed a certain favor in the eyes of the Lord even in their sinful state, but the last generation of that first dispensation found no favor at all except for Noah who "found grace in the eyes of the Lord."

If the understanding of these things is difficult, we have only to think of our own dispensation. From Calvary to the rapture is commonly known as the church age or the age of grace. In the beginning of this age,

- Christ died on an old rugged cross to purchase the church.
- "While we were yet sinners, Christ died for us."
- Our Lord ate meat with sinners that He might bring them to Himself and to salvation.
- Christ allowed the sick to touch His garment that they could be healed of their diseases.
- He came to seek and to save that which was lost.

Such compassion and love was manifested to the generation that nailed Him to a cross. Then in Revelations chapter three and verse sixteen, we hear this same Christ say to the lukewarm, Laodicean Church, "I will spew you out of my mouth."

This stern warning makes us acutely aware of a sobering fact. We are in a crisis state. This is a decisive and a crucial time. Again, "as it was in the days of Noah," God's attitude toward His people seems to have changed.

Why the change from Adam to Noah? Why the change from the first century A.D. to this present day? The change in Noah's day, and the difference in our day is the simple fact that "mixtures" were and are being produced.

As we turn our attention back to the time just prior to the flood, we find the "sons of God" becoming interested in the "daughters of men." There is debate as to who the sons of God were and who the daughters of men were.

I believe the sons of God were the descendants of the righteous man Seth. Noah was a member of this group. Some teach these to be fallen angels. There are several scriptural reasons why I do not believe this teaching. The daughters of men, I believe, were the descendants of the unrighteous man Cain.

Sethites and Cainites can co-exist on the face of the earth and not fear a flood. They can each occupy their own space and expect the forces of nature to act in a normal fashion. They can maintain their two distinct cultures and enjoy life on the earth God created. Living separate, they survived from the time of the first sin in the garden until the time of the flood.

The attraction between the sons of God and daughters of men became such that the sons of God took wives of the daughters of men. This was a dangerous thing to do. The joining together of these two cultures would surely produce something that had never before existed. A third culture was produced.

The offspring of the union of the righteous and the unrighteous were not like their father or their mother. They were a new breed of men. Giants and men of renown they were. I don't understand everything there is to know about this new third culture, but I do know that God Almighty was not pleased with it and did not like it.

I do not know how a holy man could take an unholy woman to be his wife, and produce some kind of monster man. I don't understand the biological facts of this matter. I don't understand the hereditary facts of this matter, but I fully understand the spiritual facts of this matter.

The spiritual facts are these. God is against mixtures. God does not allow seed to be mixed and hybrids be produced. The ox and ass cannot plow together in the same yoke. God hates third cultures.

As long as there is black and white, things may proceed as expected, but don't offer the gray to God and expect Him to accept it. He will not accept the mixture of compromise.

It was a fatal mistake for the generation of Noah's day to believe they could mix the two cultures present at that time, and yet have things continue as they always had been. Another mistake on their part was to forget that no matter what the condition of the world, and no matter what man might conceive and produce, Almighty God is always in control.

Maybe these pre-flood people believed that their third culture would escape the authority of God. Giants were produced. Great men were raised up, but no man-made-giant is bigger than God. No hybrid human possesses a knowledge anywhere near to the knowledge of God. And no great man is as great as our great God.

These same mistakes, and this same mentality seem to be prevalent in the late twentieth century. This generation thinks itself beyond the hand of God. Educated to a point exceeding anything known before, men are too intelligent to honor an old fashioned God.

A mixing of the cultures—the sin culture and the righteous culture—has produced a religious giant that is very well learned, very dignified, and very refined. This religious monstrosity—thinking itself to be above and beyond God—ignores God and His word.

Religious giants and great men have arose. Thinking themselves to be something, they have denied the power of God and made light of His commandments.

New rules of religion have been concocted by these hybrid, religious personalities. The old time religion is now a thing of the past. Man has become a god to himself, they say. Therefore, let everyone do as seemeth right in his own eyes.

"As it was in the days of Noah," men of this generation have also forgotten that God is in control. We know that God is not controlling the actions of many individual people today. If the almighty was governing the activities of people, their actions would be different from what they are.

We also know that God is not controlling the operations of many churches, and so called religious groups in existence today. If God was ordering the course, churches and religious groups would be more interested in seeing lost humanity saved, and in relieving the suffering of the masses than in big money and big buildings. Big business is a term that can be used to describe much of the *spiritual activity* of this age. The financial page, with its glowing reports of financial victories, has replaced the testimony page in many religious publications.

If God is not controlling the church world, and if He is not controlling individual lives, then how can we say, "God is in control?"

God is in control today the same as He was in Noah's day. He certainly was not ordering the steps of the sons of God, for had He been doing so, they would not have taken the daughters of men to be their wives. Had they been mindful of God and His will, these hybrid people would never have been produced.

How then can we say that God is in control today even as He was way back then in the first dispensation? "Even the wind and sea obey Him." The twelve disciples discovered this truth one night on the Sea of Galilee in the midst of a storm.

The generation that witnessed a flood, and the generation of today, have:

- Forgotten that mountains tremble and little hills skip like rams in His presence.
- Forgotten that He commands the sun not to move and it stands still.
- Forgotten that He makes roads across rivers and seas.

If God cannot exercise control over the lives of men with His word and commandments, then He will use His power over nature to deal with them. The flood destroyed and removed the third culture produced by mixing righteousness and unrighteousness. Likewise, to remove a lukewarm, compromised, and mixed up church, Christ has promised to "spew them out."

Can Christ remove from before Him a Laodicean church now that it has become so large and has grown so rich? Can He purge His church of the "mixture" that is in it? He certainly can and He certainly will.

When the flood waters were dried and gone from the face of the earth, not one member of that third culture existed. Likewise, after the rapture, not one member of the third culture called the lukewarm will present itself in the presence of God.

Only Noah, the man who "found grace in the eyes of the

Lord," and his wife and three sons and their wives survived.

This word grace means favor. What did Noah do to find favor in the eyes of God? The answer is very simple. So simple in fact that any man, woman, or child can duplicate it. He kept himself pure. He did not participate in the mixing fad of his day.

Noah was a Sethite man. He married a Sethite woman. They produced three Sethite sons who married Sethite daughters. These eight people who dared to be different and kept the purity of the blood line, stood on this side of the flood and saw a rainbow in the clouds.

Those of this generation who will stand firm on the Word of God, and live a life pleasing to Him, will hear Him say "well done" on that great day as the "mixers" and the third culture people hear Him say "depart from Me."

As the lukewarm are spewed out and find themselves faced with the agony of hell, Heaven with its pearly gates, golden streets, mansions, tree of life, and angel band will receive the pure in heart that they might see God.

Third cultures are a sign of crises in the church. These things tell us something is not right. As we see these things surrounding us, let us "not be weary in well doing," but rather let us rejoice that our redemption draweth nigh.

THE LORD KNOWETH THEM THAT ARE HIS.

Chapter Four
THE FIRST CHURCH OF THE FLESH

THAT THE RIGHTEOUSNESS OF THE LAW
MIGHT BE FULFILLED IN US, WHO WALK NOT
AFTER THE FLESH, BUT AFTER THE SPIRIT.
FOR THEY THAT ARE AFTER THE FLESH DO
MIND THE THINGS OF THE FLESH: BUT THEY
THAT ARE AFTER THE SPIRIT THE THINGS OF
THE SPIRIT. FOR TO BE CARNALLY MINDED
IS DEATH: BUT TO BE SPIRITUALLY MINDED
IS LIFE AND PEACE. BECAUSE THE CARNAL
MIND IS ENMITY AGAINST GOD: FOR IT IS
NOT SUBJECT TO THE LAW OF GOD, NEITHER
INDEED CAN BE. SO THEY THAT ARE IN THE
FLESH CANNOT PLEASE GOD.

~ ROMANS 8:4 8

The dominating force that moves the church determines the direction the church will take. Whether the church moves in a heavenly direction, or a worldly direction is determined solely by whether or not it is motivated by the Spirit of God, or the carnal ideas of men.

Watch the church world. Observe your own local church. See the path that these are taking, and you will know if God or man is in the pilot house.

If God's hand is on the wheel, the atmosphere will be spiritual and ministry will meet the real needs of the people. These being the need for the things of God—eternal things.

If flesh is doing the guiding and steering, then the church will move in the direction of fleshly amusement and worldly entertainment. Something for the flesh will characterize the whole program.

If there is a real desire in the hearts of Christian people today to see the church return to the "Landmarks which our fathers have set," and to see a return to the "old paths," then we must not kid ourselves. We must honestly seek a true diagnoses of the maladies that are causing the church to be in its present position.

When a certain type of machine is supposed to produce a certain product, that machine is not working properly if it is not producing that product. If a machine that is supposed to manufacture bullets for an automatic weapon begins to spit out cork stoppers for a child's pop gun, that machine is tagged "out of order," and put out of production until a technician can determine the cause of the problem and effect a cure for it.

Imagine the problems that will arise if that machine is allowed to continue in production. A soldier on a battlefield reaches for ammunition only to find he has been supplied with cork stoppers made for a child's toy gun. It would be a crisis for that poor soldier. Someone, somewhere will have to give an account for allowing that out of order machine to continue operating.

Isn't it about time we Christian people of this last day begin to act in a responsible manner, and realize that the church is not "turning out" what it is supposed to be turning out? We are equipping soldiers of the cross—whose job it is to do battle with the devil—with some sort of fleshly popgun religion instead of the power of the Holy Ghost.

- Is it any wonder that a state of crisis exist?
- Is it any wonder that the forces of evil have paid precious little attention to our preaching and praying?
- Are we surprised when our singing and worship

creates no stir in hell?

Let's show a little maturity, admit our problem, accept our blame, and shoulder the responsibility for it.

The problem is that the flesh has taken the rulership of the church from the Spirit, and has expected God to accept our tainted sacrifice and to bless it. History—church as well as secular—tells us that God has never accepted the works of the flesh from any person or group of people. Though it has been tried many times in the past, and is currently being tried today, it has never been accepted by God.

Cain brought an unacceptable sacrifice to his altar only to discover that the fire of God would not fall on it. This was a mistake, but it was not the worst mistake that Cain made. His worse mistake was in failing to admit that his offering was unacceptable, and then repent and bring a proper sacrifice.

Many today are making Cain's first mistake. God help them not to make his second one. Help us, oh God, to realize that the carnal mind is enmity with you, and that by acting after the motivation of the flesh we become your enemies instead of your sons.

Only those who are "led by the spirit" are recognized as the sons of God. Many know this truth, yet continue to be directed by the flesh.

Every generation has a religious distinction. Some teaching, or revelation prevails, and the prevailing teaching or revelation marks that particular generation. In the time of Martin Luther, the time now called the reformation, the prevailing teaching was that "The just shall live by faith." Out of this era was born Protestantism. The time of John Wesley is remembered as the time of evangelism, and the circuit riding preachers. Charles Finney, D.L. Moody, Billy Sunday, and others distinguished themselves in great revival crusades.

There was a period of several years in this twentieth century when the revival movement was not only identified by the number of souls being saved, but also by the message and the practice of divine healing.

When we look at our present generation, we must conclude and admit that the religious distinction now is the strong influence of flesh and carnality over a vast majority of the activities that are supposed to be spiritual. Surely this day will have to be recorded in the pages of church history as the day of fleshly motivation.

It is a terrible mistake, but this generation has made it.

To think that spiritual ends can be achieved by fleshly means borders on some kind of religious insanity. That it's "Not by might nor by power but by My spirit" is one of God's unchangeable laws that this generation has forgotten.

Ignoring the fact that "Whatsoever a man soweth that shall he also reap," we have hoped for a spiritual harvest after having sown the flesh. It will not happen. It cannot happen. If it did happen, God's word would not be the "Same yesterday, today, and forever."

It would be just as easy for the sun to rise in the west and set in the east as it would be to sow fleshly seed, and to reap spiritual fruit. The same God that put the sun on its course of rising in the east and setting in the west said, "If we sow to the flesh we shall after the flesh reap corruption." It is God's law, it cannot change. We have—in this generation—already begun to reap corruption.

Even Abraham, that great man of God, was led to believe that flesh could please God, and the seed of flesh could produce the promise of God. Let's consider and compare the Old Testament story of Abraham, Sarah, Hagar, Ishmael, and Isaac with the religious happenings of our time.

It all began when God made Abraham a promise. God promised this man who had no children a son. A promise of a son to a man who has never fathered a child would have to be a very exciting thing. Imagine the feeling of joy as the voice of the Lord speaks such wonderful words to this man and his wife Sarah.

God's promises are always exciting. The level of expectancy and enthusiasm is greatly elevated when a person or group of persons are made aware that they are about to be the recipients of the fulfillment of a promise from God. At times and under certain circumstances, this rise in excitement and enthusiasm can be dangerous. Although I am sure God wants His people to be thrilled concerning His promises, He does not want them to allow this thrill and elation to cause them to become impatient and fleshly minded.

A lack of patience has caused many, Abraham—Sarah included—to do foolish things trying to "help" God fulfill His promises.

Our generation is certainly in the position to receive the fulfillment of many of the promises of God. Perhaps no generation—with the possible exception of the one that was alive at the time of the birth of Christ—has ever been in a position to receive the fulfillment of more of the promises of God than this present one.

Think about this fact for a moment. Think about the promises and prophecies that have come to pass in the last fifty years or so. One of the greatest of these being the re-gathering of Israel to the land of Palestine.

Ezekiel's vision of the valley of dry bones is no longer a mystery. We have witnessed "bone coming to his bone" and have watched as the nation of Israel has stood to its feet as "a mighty army." The gospel of the kingdom has circled the globe. Is there any corner of the world today that is out of reach of the gospel? Modern advances in communication technology make it possible to blanket our earth with the gospel. These are only two examples. There are many others.

Now, let us consider some of the promises that we are yet expecting to come to pass in our day. First, we have a promise of the outpouring of the spirit on "all flesh." On the male and the female. On the young and the old. On the members of every race and color. We are told by the prophet Joel, and the apostle Peter that dreams and visions would accompany this outpouring of the spirit. Peter told us on the day of Pentecost—immediately after the believers had been filled with the Holy Ghost and every one of them had spoken in tongues—"This is that which was spoken by the prophet Joel." So we are right to believe that the outpouring of the spirit is to include the evidence of "speaking in other tongues."

"All flesh" means all flesh. Not just those who are members of the traditional Pentecostal ranks. Not just the ones who were once called holy rollers by the nominal, main line churches, but all flesh. Signs, wonders, and miracles are to be a part of the latter day out pouring. Isn't this exciting! Isn't this wonderful! We are the generation of promise. We are going to see a mighty outpouring of God's spirit on all flesh.

We also have the promise of that great event, the catching away of the church, commonly called the rapture. What could be better than this? What could be better than to live in the generation that is fully expecting the return of our Lord to resurrect our loved ones who died in the faith, bring them forth from the graves, and then catch the living saints away from this earth, give us all new bodies and take us home with Him. All tears shall be wiped away from our eyes. All pain and suffering will be gone. Death will be abolished. It is certainly an exciting promise.

Then will come that awful time known as the Great Tribulation. Antichrist will be revealed. The terrible wrath of God—we find recorded in the book of the Revelations—will be poured out on the Beast and the world. This is not something to get excited about being a part of, but it is surely something to be excited about missing out on.

Armageddon is coming. That battle of all battles will be fought between the forces of Christ and Antichrist. We are told in scripture how the blood will run so deep it will touch the horses bridle. Christ will overcome all the forces of evil at that time. I am thrilled at the thought of riding out of Heaven on a white horse to help celebrate our Lord's victory over evil at the battle of Armageddon.

And then the Millennium is coming. For one thousand years Christ will rule this earth as He sits on the throne of David. The lamb shall lay down with the lion. The lion will eat grass with the ox. Children will play near the hole of the asp and near the crocodile den. Swords will be beaten into plowshares. Men will learn war no more. Nothing shall by any means hurt or destroy. Then we will know the meaning of that glorious old hymn that says, *there will be peace in the valley for me*. This is something to rejoice about.

When we consider all these great promises it is almost impossible to contain ourselves. To think that in our lifetime these things are very likely to happen. When we study scripture and compare scripture with things that are occurring all around us, we can come to no other conclusion than the fact that this is the last days, and we are the generation that will witness the fulfillment of the last day prophecies.

There has been a great stir in religious circles in the past few years. This stir has been brought about by the very fact that we recognize, and realize we are to be the recipients of many great and precious promises:

- A mighty Holy Ghost outpouring with signs following,
- The resurrection of the dead,
- The catching away of the saints,
- A promise of escape from the Great Tribulation,
- Victory at Armageddon, and a part in the Millennium.

The realization that we are to witness such things is enough to do for us what the promise of a son did to Abraham and for Abraham.

When Abraham received his promise and realized that something wonderful was about to happen, it had a profound effect on him and his entire house. Things were never the same from that day forward. It was a turning point in his life. For many years he had lived a life of contentment and submission to God. In his dealings with God and with others—such as his nephew Lot— he had kept his flesh under subjection, and he had walked humbly and honestly before God and men.

But now the promise excites him, and he is about to act in a manner in which he has never acted before. Elated over the promise of a son, he's persuaded to use the facilities of the flesh to help bring about the fulfillment of the promise of God. This man who for many years has trusted and waited patiently on God—now through his excitement over the promise given him—becomes impatient.

This impatience leads to a certain amount of doubt. This doubt leads to certain questions. I can imagine Abraham and Sarah must have discussed among themselves, and questioned each other as to how God would be able to do such a thing as to bring a child from her dead womb. These discussions and questions brought them to a logical and natural conclusion. This conclusion being that it would be impossible for the promise to come to pass without some help from the flesh.

A plan was devised to help God. God must have a little help from the flesh if this thing is going to be. This was the conclusion to which Abraham and his wife Sarah arrived. The only way for a son to be born and the promise be fulfilled, is to bring in another woman, Hagar, and have Abraham lie with her so that she might conceive and bear him a son.

I don't think this was a hurried decision, or a spur of the moment thing. Perhaps several months having passed since the promise was given, discouragement began to set in. No doubt it seemed to Abraham and Sarah that something was wrong. There was no questioning the promise, for of this they were sure. God had spoken. A son was promised and there would be a son for God cannot lie. But how could it be? What can be done? It was perhaps at this time that the plan to "help God" was born.

We can be sure of one thing. Their intentions were good. There were no thoughts of hindering God or getting in the way of His plan. They were only trying to help. But?

- Does God need any help?
- Is God not able to be God?
- Is there a weakness found in Him?
- Does God make promises that He is unable to keep?
- Do prophecies flow forth from the mouth of God

that the hand of God is too feeble to bring to pass? Apparently Abraham and Sarah thought so.

God needs no help being God. His power is sufficient to His word. If God needed help being God, who would be qualified for the job?

This is not to say that God does not need men and women in His service. He certainly does for He has chosen human beings be His servants. However, He needs only submission and a willing and obedient heart. If He can find a clean vessel, He is well able to fill it with His spirit, and use it for His glory. •

God did not need Abraham's fleshly help. All He needed was for Abraham to walk uprightly and humbly before Him, and wait on His promise.

This wrong thinking caused a great error to be committed. An act of fleshly indulgence, the sin of adultery, transpired in order to "help God" fulfill a spiritual promise. Fleshly seed was sown with the hope of reaping a spiritual harvest.

It did not work. Fleshly seed was sown. A son was born, but he was not the promised son. He was a son after the flesh. Flesh begets flesh. It always has, and it always will. Spiritual things are only produced as spiritual seed is sown. Spirit begets spirit.

This very thing has happened in our day. The process has been repeated. The picture has been reproduced. The church of our day, realizing we are the generation of promise, and becoming impatient with God's tarrying, we have tried to "help God."

This generation began to realize we are the generation of promise during and nearing the end of World War II. That new weapon of mass destruction—the atomic bomb—was dropped on two cities of Japan in August, 1945 killing approximately 132,000 people. We knew Armageddon was on its way.

It was preached by many that this was the road to Armageddon. Surely, it was not far away. With a zeal perhaps never equaled before, men were warned to flee the wrath to come.

I think the preachers of 1945 were right. This was the beginning of the road to Armageddon. The only problem being that this road has been a lot longer than it was thought to be.

Three years later, when Ezekiel's vision of the valley of dry bones was fulfilled, and the nation of Israel returned to its homeland of Palestine, the world watched as the fig tree began to bud and bring forth leaves. Our eyes were opened to the fact, "This generation shall not pass until all things be fulfilled."

The message was preached. This was a sign of the rapture. The Lord is coming. Surely any day now the eastern skies will open and Jesus will appear to catch away His waiting bride. Behold the cry, "The Bridegroom cometh, go ye out to meet Him," will soon be heard.

The promise of the return of our Lord for His church was placed before our eyes very vividly. This re-gathering of Israel to its homeland was one of the greatest signs that this blessed event was soon to happen. There was a zeal. There was an excitement. The Lord is coming! Get ready! Stay ready! Be ready at all times! These were the cries that were heard over and over in 1948, and the years that followed.

The preachers were right. The message was right. This was the beginning of the end. The rapture is eminent. But the promise has been longer in coming than what any of the preachers thought.

The rise of Antichrist has been a favorite sermon topic for many years. Especially since the time of Adolf Hitler. This evil man with no conscience, who had thousands of Jews destroyed for the sake of prejudice and politics, must surely be "the man of sin." This message was preached. The "son of perdition" had arrived on the scene. But then Hitler was gone.

In 1960, the United States of America elected a man to the office of President who was of the Catholic faith. The Antichrist message was once again renewed with an evangelistic fervor. Rome, the city of seven hills, the Vatican with its great power, the Catholic Church with its worldwide influence, a president of the Catholic persuasion, add all these factors together and who could this man be but the Antichrist?

Then there was that day in Dallas. The firing of a rifle. The president slumping forward in the limousine. The vice president taking the oath of office on an airplane.

Antichrist is coming. There will be a "man of sin" revealed. This message is true, but it has taken longer to come to pass than anyone ever imagined.

Also, at about the same time, near the end of World War II, there arose a great revival movement across our land. The great crusades brought thousands to the saving knowledge of Christ. Signs, wonders, and great miracles of healing were wrought. This surely must be the final fulfillment of the prophecies of Joel, the preachers said. The spirit will now be poured out on all flesh. People from every religious walk will accept the experience of the second chapter of Acts. Pentecost and the Pentecostal blessing will now be embraced even by those who have traditionally opposed it.

This was the thought pattern of the ones involved in this great awakening. The message was once again proclaimed, "This is that." This is the fulfillment of the "in the last days" prophecy. But by the time the decade of the sixties was coming to a close, we were made aware of this fact; we would have to wait a little longer for "the promised son."

Over all these promises and prophecies there had been an initial reaction of great excitement and enthusiasm. When this excitement and enthusiasm found itself in a position of waiting and impatience questions and doubt arose in the heart of the church. The same as had arisen in the heart of Abraham long ago.

Yes, it happened. Just as Abraham and Sarah decided God needed help, the church world began to devise ways to help God keep His promises.

Just as Abraham and Sarah's decision to turn to the arm of flesh to help God produce a son, so the decision of some in this generation to help God by the works of the flesh has produced a great religious commotion.

Abraham and Sarah's action did bring a son to birth, but he was not the promised son. He was not Isaac. They had produced Ishmael. A wild man. Not a spiritual man, but a man of the flesh.

There was no way they could have ever dreamed or imagined the trouble the "man after the flesh" was going to cause.

We have witnessed the birth of the Ishmael church.

A church born out of a feeling of frustration and impatience. A church conceived in the minds of some religious philosophers and thinkers. A church attempting to use fleshly means to produce spiritual ends. Someone has forgotten that Jesus told Nicodemus, "That which is born of the flesh is flesh, and that which is born of the spirit is spirit."

This movement that I refer to as The First Church of The Flesh, has become commonly known as the *Charismatic Movement* or the *Neo-Pentecostal Movement*. Trying to force something to happen, whether it be of God or not, is a characteristic of the movement.

Such things as trying to force the rapture to take place by predicting a date and a time has become too common. It may be that these rapture-forecasters think that the Lord will accept their Ishmael-rapture and return for His people.

By feeding data into computers and manipulating men's names to make them total up to and equal 666, men of the last forty or so years have introduced many "Ishmael Antichrist" to the world, perhaps thinking that God would honor their efforts and let it be so.

Unable—because of sin in the camp—to see an outpouring of the Holy Ghost in revivals, crusades and church services, flesh has done its work. When—because of sin and a lack of commitment and dedication to God and Godly principles—people are not able to receive a true infilling of the Holy Ghost, they are given a so called prayer language. Unable to wait for the promise, they are taught tongues by someone having them "repeat after me." God— it seems—needs a little help baptizing His children in the Spirit.

Surely we know this is not the way it was on the Day of Pentecost. It could not have happened in this manner in Topeka, Kansas, in 1901.

These people must know they are operating in the flesh and after a fleshly manner. I am sure they do. They are only hoping that if God hears them "speaking in tongues," He will honor this by sending the Holy Ghost. But the truth is this. God does not accept our Ishmaels.

Men and women who are unable to receive divine healing for their bodies, whatever the reason, are taught to make positive confessions and deny the very fact that they are sick. God is supposed to hear their confession, "no pain in Jesus name," and honor it with divine healing virtue.

Positive confessions are made for houses, cars, and countless other things in the hope that our fleshly talk will be honored with a spiritual blessing.

In the initial excitement over the birth of Ishmael, it seems the promise has come. As the years passed, it became evident that something was wrong.

We are at that place today. The knowledge that something is wrong is inescapable.

- Too many predictions without fulfillment.
- Too much speaking in tongues with too little fruit of the spirit.
- Too much confessing "no pain in Jesus name" with too little evidence of healing.

These facts should open the eyes of many to the fact that something is dreadfully wrong.

Abraham tried in every way to persuade God to accept Ishmael. He even circumcised him. He prayed and asked God to let him stand before him.

God refused. He would accept nothing that was after the flesh.

When God's time came, Isaac, the son of promise was born. Now Abraham has two sons. He has a son after the flesh, and a son after the spirit. This situation has the smell of trouble. These two, fleshly and spiritual, will not be able to dwell together.

This generation of promise will see the fulfillment of all the promises of God that pertain to it. Nothing can stop this from happening.

Ishmael cannot prevent Isaac from being born.

The so called Charismatic Movement, or the Neo-Pentecostal Movement cannot and will not stop a true fulfillment of the promise of an outpouring of the spirit in the last days.

- The First Church of The Flesh will not stop God from raising up a genuine, Holy Ghost church.
- The false "forecasters" will not prevent a real rapture.
- Tongue talking imitators cannot stop a real baptism in the Holy Ghost with the evidence of speaking in other tongues.
- The "no pain in Jesus name" crowd will not rob us of the divine healing purchased for us through the stripes that were placed on Jesus' back.
- The birth of Ishmael will not cancel the birth of Isaac.
- The false will not be greater than the real.
- The imposter will not receive the blessing of the heir.

Abraham was instructed to give Ishmael and his mother bread and water, and send them away.

If we can learn the lesson that is here for us, separate ourselves from the works of the flesh, pray through, and wait on God then we can see and become a part of the promise. **"IN THE LAST DAYS SAYS GOD, I WILL POUR OUT OF MY SPIRIT ON ALL FLESH."**

Chapter Five
PROPHETS FOR PROFITS

NO MAN CAN SERVE TWO MASTERS: FOR
EITHER HE WILL HATE THE ONE, AND LOVE
THE OTHER: OR ELSE HE WILL HOLD TO THE
ONE, AND DESPISE THE OTHER. YE CANNOT
SERVE GOD AND MAMMON.
~ MATTHEW 6:42

Webster's New World Dictionary, Second College Edition, gives the definition of the word mammon: *Riches regarded as an object of worship and greedy pursuit.*

The role money and riches have played in the realm of religion and the churches is a topic that cannot be overlooked as we discuss the present state and condition of the church.

In the previous chapter, we looked at the direction the church has taken as it has been ruled by the flesh. In this chapter we shall see—at least in part—the reason that flesh and carnality have such an interest in the things of the spirit.

With promises of material blessings, as well as spiritual ones—*Beloved, I wish above all things that thou mayest prosper and be in health, even as thy soul prospereth*—it is no wonder that carnal minded men have turned to religion as a way to wealth and prosperity.

With the doctrine of blessings coming as a reward for giving, *It is more blessed to give than to receive* and *Give and it shall be given unto you* being one of the fundamental teachings of God's word, it is no wonder that con men and charlatans have appeared on the stage of Christianity.

Using these Biblical principles as text, these are teaching a false doctrine of prosperity. People looking for an easy road to prosperity are hearing them, believing them, and supporting them by sending them money under the name of a blessing plan, seed faith, or some other wild scheme.

Cards, letters, and telephone calls go out to hundreds of thousands every month promising them every imaginable thing in return for a love gift sent to their address. They assure their donors that the gift is for the Lord and His work, but they want it sent to their P.O. Box.

The sad fact is, while these are teaching the principles of giving in order to take advantage of people, and these same people are giving in order to receive some mystical blessing in return, the real work of God suffers.

Many are the monuments that have been built to men while the church has in many instances gone lacking. Multi-million dollar resorts, complete with playgrounds, swimming pools, and hotels have been built while the local church that many of the donors attend cannot afford a new roof or paint for their buildings.

Men of questionable reputation are living in unparalleled luxury from the tithes and offerings of church members. Meanwhile, local pastors that visit them when they are sick and in need, that preach the funerals of their deceased loved ones, and dedicate their newborn babies are praying for food to feed their families. They struggle to make ends meet from month to month while others in places far removed from the actual field of labor are living in high style.

We have been exposed to the religion of the dollar for several years now. Those who prophesy for profit have been around long enough for people to see through their schemes. Most of the big money ministries are now reeling from the loss of respect and the loss of revenue. The rivers of cash are not flowing now as they have done in the past in many cases.

It is no surprise that this financial drought has come. The amazing thing is the length of time it has taken for the public to see through the thin veneer of righteousness. Many have covered their actual motives with trying to appear spiritual. Their greed has shown through. No trick, scheme, or gimmick has been left out. If it could be imagined, it has been tried.

Men with great names and reputations have made themselves appear as fools as their reasons for ministry have shifted from "exhorting" to "extorting."

One man whose name became a household word because of the anointing of the Holy Ghost on his life and ministry, for some reason lost that anointing and changed his entire operation.

It is good to watch closely those who suddenly have their ministry changed by some vision or revelation from the Lord. The gifts and calling of God are without repentance.

Going from being a mighty Holy Ghost evangelist to being a big business executive; his priorities changed, his motives changed, and his methods changed.

His priorities were to build the kingdom of God. Now it's to build great buildings on which to inscribe his name.

His motives were that lost men might be saved, sick men might be healed, and those bound by Satan might be delivered. Now it's some kind of bloated statistic and head count that he might appear more successful that his competitor. This apparent success brings in more money.

His methods were the preaching of the unadulterated Word of God and obedience to that Word, so that miracles, signs and wonders might be wrought to the glory of God. Now the methods being used are tricks, gimmicks, and cheap psychology.

To sell the blessing of God borders on blasphemy. To tell simple minded and gullible souls that the larger the gift they send the larger the heavenly package of blessings will be when it is delivered to their door, is nothing less than an insult to God, and a denial of the truth of the Bible from which he quotes.

69

God is even accused of holding this man "hostage," with the threat to kill him, if he doesn't raise a certain amount of money by a certain time.

I read in the Bible where Felix—a servant of Satan—held the apostle Paul in prison hoping that money would be given him for Paul's release, but I cannot imagine that another of the apostles would hold Paul hostage. It would be strange indeed if this great man of God wrote a letter to Timothy begging him to raise thousands of dollars to pay in ransom for his release from Peter, or James, or John.

Peter, James, and John were men of God, they would never do a thing such as this, some would say. If God's men would not do such a thing, then surely God Himself would not.

He will not.

He did not.

It was a "prophet prophesying for profit." Leaving the pulpit of the evangelist and taking to the desk of the executive, he became a "Prophet for Profit."

This is one of the devil's tricks that has been on the books for a long time. It's not a new thing for Satan to look for a man of God who prophesies for edification of the kingdom of God that he can change into a "Prophet for Profit."

His reason for this is not to make the prophet rich, but to create a condition of crisis in the church so that the church can be stopped, or at least hindered and slowed down.

Consider the prophet Balaam. Balaam was a man with quite a reputation. It was said that whoever "Balaam blessed was blessed and whoever Balaam cursed was cursed." Is it any wonder that when the enemy of Israel—in this case it was Balak—looked for one to cause crisis and chaos in the camp of Israel, that he turned to Balaam?

"Cause a curse to come on the people of God and you will become wealthy." This was the message Balak sent to Balaam. What a temptation.

Balaam resisted and refused Balak's first offer. Balak, whose name means devastator, was determined and did not give up easily. Men with higher rank, and carrying greater promises of wealth and honor were sent to Balaam. At this point Balaam made a terrible mistake. He talked to God again about this matter. Already God had commanded him not to go with these men. Balaam must have thought that perhaps God would change His mind and alter His word. With this much wealth and honor at stake it was worth a try.

Did God change His mind? Did God alter His word? No! He is the same yesterday, today and forever. He cannot change.

Balaam did not receive a new direction for his ministry of prophesy, but he did show us one profound truth. If a body wants to do something bad enough, God will allow it.

These one hundred eighty degree turns that many ministers and ministries have taken, from righteousness to unrighteousness, from conservatism to liberalism, from power to politics, and from glory to gold, cannot be divinely directed by God. They are simply men walking after their own lust. God does not sanction it. He only allows it because men are free to choose the path they take in this life.

There is absolutely no way that God would send a man on a mission, such as the one Balaam was going on, when the sole purpose of that mission was to separate God from His people. God is not the author of confusion.

God did not ordain nor inspire men of our day to act in ways that have led to disgrace, not only for them, but for the entire kingdom of God.

We have watched as men—proclaiming themselves to be sent from God—have wrought havoc in the church. Confusion, dissention, and division have come to the body of Christ in the name of Christ. Men have been convicted and sentenced for criminal acts which they have committed while supposedly being under the anointing of the Holy Ghost.

These things have happened because like Balaam, once the offer of wealth and honor has been presented to them it becomes an obsession to their minds, blinding, deceiving, and leading them astray. Planning and scheming, they try to come up with a way to "worship God and mammon." This is impossible. A choice must be made. Many, to their own hurt and ruin, have made the wrong choice.

Balaam knew that he could not put a curse from God on the people of God no matter how great the reward he was offered. He could never separate God from His people. God would never break or violate the promises He had made to Abraham, Isaac, and Jacob. God cannot be bought or sold.

However, with an eye on the reward, he devised a plan that would cause the people to separate themselves from God. He counseled Balak and had him offer something for the flesh to the Israelites.

Invite them to worship your gods with you. Introduce them to idolatry. Give to them your daughters for fleshly pleasure, offer them joy and happiness. Promise them excitement. Show to them the way to fleshly fulfillment, and they will respond to you and your plan.

Don't call it sin. That would frighten them. Don't call it adultery. That would enlighten them. Don't call it an abomination. That would convict them. It has to be called a plan. A blessing plan. A prosperity plan.

The plan was devised and the offer was made. Israel fell for it. Without regard to what was right or wrong, they followed a plan that would bring them carnal pleasure and fleshly rewards. The results being thousands of Israelites slain as the wrath of God was poured out on them. Balaam also perished.

A prophet who desired profit more than life and who lusted after the rewards of the world, paid a dear price. He lost his respect. He lost his integrity. He lost his ministry. He lost his life. It's terrible to see what happened to this once respectable and respected man when he tried to serve God and mammon. It's also terrible to see what happened to the children of Israel who followed him in his folly.

How sad it is when men who have gained great respect through the power and anointing of God on their lives, begin to regard riches as an object of worship and teach men so. The blind lead the blind, and they both fall into the ditch.

In this story of Balaam and Balak, things had gotten into a reverse order. Balaam should have been with God's people in their conflict with Balak instead of standing on a mountain top with Balak looking down into the camp of Israel trying to figure out a way to make personal gain at the expense of God's people.

We see things in reverse order in the church world today. In the days of Elijah, Elisha, John the Baptist, and all the prophets of old, things were not as they are today.

The people needed the prophets. The prophets did not get up on a stump and tell the people how they needed them and their support. These men of God never said, "If you don't give to me I will lose this ministry that God has given me." Can you imagine Moses saying to the children of Israel, "Bring me all your gold and all your silver, for if you refuse to do so I will lose my calling and you won't have me to lead you?" My mind cannot even imagine such in its wildest dreams.

Moses would never have pulled such a caper, but a fellow who was trying to establish and support a false worship to a golden calf asked for their gold.

Gold that was brought out of Egypt for the purpose of being used in God's tabernacle was wasted on a golden calf. Only the records of Heaven will reveal how much of God's gold, that should've been used in God's work, has gone into some backslid preacher's golden calf—a building with that preachers name on it.

The people of old needed the prophets. They blessed the prophets with material things because they felt a need for the prophet to be in their presence.

A widow in the city of Zarepath fed Elijah for a period of time during a famine. She fed him from a meal barrel that never ran out, and a cruse of oil that never went dry. She needed that man of God in her house. Without his presence there, she and her son would have ran out of food.

There came a day when this widow's son died. She needed the prophet. The prophet was available. That's more than we can say about some of the religious con-artists of today. Where are they when the people who have supported them are in trouble? The deceased son was restored to life.

The story of Naaman the leper, and the prophet Elisha is an example of the proper order of things. Naaman takes a journey to the prophet's house because the prophet has what Naaman needs.

In our society today, it's the other way around. The prophets of mammon buy television time to come into the homes of the people, because the people have something the prophet needs—money.

It's such a slick sell. Give me money and you will be healed. Make a pledge and you will be blessed. Deed your property to my ministry, and God will give you a better piece of property in return. How disgusting!

Elisha asked nothing of Naaman before he told him to dip seven times in the river Jordan, and would receive nothing at his hand after he was healed of his leprosy. He would not prophesy for profit.

The servant of this man of God saw a golden opportunity to cash in on the mighty miracle of healing. He followed Naaman down the road, overtook him, and asked for money. Watch out for the man of religion who tracks you down by mail, telephone, radio, or television to tell you that God wants you to contribute to his golden calf. When he tells you that God has said for you to send him a thousand dollars or some other fixed amount, then be warned. The wolf in sheep's clothing seeks a prey.

Giving to support the work of God, and to support those doing the work of God is right and honorable. God will surely bless those who do so, but God's blessings are not for sale. They cannot be bought or sold. Give because you love God, and because you love God's work, not because you love yourself, and want to reap a million dollar harvest for your one hundred dollar seed faith that you have sown. Jesus said if we give a cup of cold water in the name of a disciple, we would not lose our reward.

Gehazi—that poor misguided servant of Elisha—was stricken with the leprosy of Naaman. A man who lived in the presence of a prophet of God, who saw many miracles wrought by the power of God at the hands of that prophet, and who might one day have the mantle of the prophet passed on to him, dies a miserable death in a state of disgrace.

The greatness of a preacher is often judged by the building that he preaches in, the crowds that follow him, or the clothes he wears. Many times, all these things take priority over the spiritual things because of this unrighteous judgment. It's not whether or not a man prays until he touches Heaven, but whether or not he can motivate a crowd.

- Can he thrill the audience?
- Does he have charisma?
- Can he tell fantastic stories about himself?
- Can he entertain the people?

These seem to be some of the most important qualifications of the ministry today.

The New Testament tells about a man who did not have a church building. This man preached in the wilderness. His meat was locust and wild honey. No doubt, he drank water from the Jordan River. No fine, three-piece, tailor made, suit for this preacher. He wore a suit of camel's hair and a leather girdle. Some went out to see him and evidently came back disappointed for Jesus asked them, "What went you out to see, a reed shaken in the wind?" This prophet did not have much charisma, evidently. He called his crowd a generation of vipers. A bunch of snakes! That's what he called them! Now that would be enough to get his credentials pulled in a lot of organizations today.

Half of his service was not spent taking up money. He did not ask his crowd to bring their watches, and diamonds, and pearls, and car titles, and land deeds, and certificates of deposits, and wills and place them in a hollow log out there somewhere in the wilderness so he could sell them to the pawn shop at the end of the revival. No, all he asked those attending his meeting to bring was proof that they had repented.

What kind of preacher was this? Where did he come from and why was he allowed to preach? John the Baptist was the forerunner of Christ. His job was to prepare the way of the Lord, and to make His paths straight.

He was not a prophet for profit. He never got rich with this world's goods. He never won a popularity contest in this world. In fact his earthly reward for his message was to have his head removed from his body. But he had the greatest reward, and highest compliment a man could have when Jesus Christ Himself said, "There was never a greater born of woman than John."

A crowd pleasing message, or a blessing plan with a get rich quick scheme will never take a person where that statement of Jesus took John the Baptist.

Prophets for profits with their psychology, their bribery, and their unscriptural promises, have contributed greatly to the crisis that the church finds itself in today. Thousands have lost faith in Christ as they have lost faith in these false prophets.

Many today believe that Christianity is a hoax. They made a faith pledge to some greedy man and did not receive the promised reward.

Churches are being robbed of tithes and offerings. These people feel that to give to the true church would be the same as to give to these men.

It's time for the true church, and real men and women of God to pray through, stand up, and show the world there is a difference.

There is a difference between the holy and the vile.

There is a difference between the ministers who minister for personal gain and those who have a burden to do the work of the Lord no matter the cost to them.

It's time to show the world the difference.

Money certainly played a part in the early church. Many in Jerusalem sold their possessions, brought the money, and laid it at the apostle's feet that it might be used as they saw fit in the kingdom of God. There were widows to be fed, and orphans to be attended to. There was a need for finances, and God supplied that need by moving on the hearts of some of His people.

Religious work of today must have finances. The bills have to be paid, but let's get one thing straight in our minds, we must use money to build the kingdom of God. We must not use God's name to build a fortune, or to build monuments to some man.

When this generation grasps this truth, and begins to use money to the glory of God—instead of using God to the glory of money—then we will see the crisis begin to pass.

This generation may see hard economic times ahead. Money and finances may become scarce. Religious businesses will go out of business. Some already have. Schools have closed. Hospitals have ceased to operate. So called ministries have folded as the creditors came calling.

We may see even more of this sort of thing in the future, but God owns the cattle on a thousand hills. The silver is His, and the gold is His. God will never go broke. His assets are heavenly, not earthly. Nothing on this planet can cause Him to go broke. If the true church runs out of money—earthly money—she can still look at the lame men lying at our gates and say, "Silver and gold have I none, but such as I have give I thee, in the name of Jesus rise up and walk."

Money can't buy that miracle. That miracle cannot be produced by prophets prophesying for profit. That miracle can only be produced by men and women of God who have something to offer people. Those who look on lost, dying, and hurting humanity with a desire to do something for that poor soul instead of seeing that suffering one as another dollar in their pocket.

DELIVER US FROM THE PROPHETS FOR PROFITS AND SEND A REVIVAL, OH GOD.

Chapter Six
THE DOOR THE HOLY GHOST WOULD NOT OPEN

PETER THEREFORE WAS KEPT IN PRISON
BUT PRAYER WAS MADE, WITHOUT CEASING
OF THE CHURCH UNTO GOD FOR HIM. BUT
PETER CONTINUED KNOCKING: AND WHEN
THEY HAD OPENED THE DOOR, AND SAW
HIM THEY WERE ASTONISHED.
~ ACTS 12:5, 16

Throughout this book, the crisis state of the church has been exposed and examined. An attempt has been made to be opened minded and honest. A whitewash job to hide the flaws is not what's needed at this point in time. We are much too close to the end for that. The problems must be faced head on if we intend to solve them.

This has been the intent of this writing up to this point. Now as any good doctor would do, after having found the problem and making a proper diagnosis, we must prescribe a remedy and begin to effect a cure.

Biblical examples have been used to show us the reasons the church has declined, and found herself in a crisis state. Using examples such as Samson, Daniel, Abraham, and others as spiritual mirrors, we have been able to see ourselves. Facing spiritual blindness with Samson, standing in the face of legalized sin with

Daniel, and fighting against the flesh with Abraham, we now find ourselves needing help desperately.

- Is there any help to turn to?
- Is there any hope?
- Have we gone too far in the wrong direction?
- Have we sunk too low to be rescued?

Again, we turn to Biblical examples for answers to these questions.

- Samson was restored.
- Daniel persevered.
- Abraham received his promised son after all.
- There is hope.
- There is a source of help.
- There is a way out of our dilemma.

The early church found itself in a severe crisis in the twelfth chapter of the book of Acts. Help was found. A great victory was won. The people of that hour did not cower down in the face of opposition, throw up their hands and say, "It's no use to try." They found a way out of their crisis. They found a remedy. They broke the powers of evil that were trying to destroy the church in its infancy. They turned their mourning into shouting. Sorrow was turned into joy. Weeping was changed to laughter.

From this group of believers, we can be inspired to do the same thing. The first generation of Christians—by their actions in a time of trouble—provide an example for those of us who find ourselves in the last days of the church. Let's be stirred to action now, as we look into what they did then.

The situation in Jerusalem had become very grave for the followers of Christ. After Pentecost—with the believers all full of the Holy Ghost—the conversion of men and women to Christ, and the signs and wonders that followed them put this city in an uproar. The forces of evil were not content to sit idly by and see the religious, social, and political tide turn in favor of Christianity. So trouble began to arise. As the social, religious, and political leaders began to feel threatened by this new religion, a consensus was reached that something must be done and done fast to stop this crowd and their message.

The solution to the problem—it was agreed upon—was to destroy the leadership. If the shepherd is destroyed the sheep will be scattered and fall prey to the beast of the forest.

This thinking sounds strangely familiar to our ears today. It's the leadership, the successful preacher, the big names in religion that are being attacked by the enemy. Not all of them have fallen, but enough have to put the church in a very acute position. Sheep are being scattered. A loss of faith and a certain confusion has gripped the hearts of many. All this is taking place while many professed Christians sleep on a church pew—unconcerned about what is going on around them.

The answer today is the same as it was in Jerusalem in the first days of the church. The answer lies with the body of believers. Not the leadership. If we are to come through this crisis victorious, then those sleeping on the pew must awaken and arouse from their slumber. The leadership is being attacked, and the church must rise to the occasion and do battle with the forces of evil.

In Jerusalem the enemy started at the top. Herod—the scripture says—began to vex certain of the church. Certain ones were nagged, harassed, embarrassed, anything to try to discourage them. Illegal arrest, confiscation of property, imprisonment and public mockery, were no doubt tried along with many other things to stop them.

When this vexation did not work, then Herod turned to more drastic measures. Verse two, of chapter twelve, tells us that he killed James, the brother of John, with the sword. James was not an usher or a doorkeeper in the house of God, he was among the first of the original twelve to be chosen by Jesus. If a doorkeeper is killed there will be mourning over him, but the work of the church will be affected very little. If one of the original twelve apostles is murdered, that will have a different effect.

It's not hard to imagine the effect this crime had on the young church. Fear and dread settled over it like a cloud. Faith was weakened. Morale was damaged. Crisis had come to the church.

Now, let's learn a great truth about Satan. Once he starts a campaign to destroy, there will be no stopping until someone stops him.

He will not kill James and stop there. Of this we can be sure. He proceeded to take Peter also with the intent to kill him. The murder of James pleased the Jews, so the murder of Peter should really elate them.

Where will it stop? When will it stop? These are questions that were surely on the minds of the early Christians.

They are also questions being asked by Christians of this generation. The answer is the exact same now as it was then. **Satan will stop when the church decides to stop him.**

As soon as this group of early Christians decided that Herod had killed enough of the apostles, then something was done to stop him.

As soon as the Christians of this last day decide that the church has been damaged enough by all these scandals and all the things that Satan is doing, then war can be waged and a victory can be won.

There is no reference to a prayer meeting when certain of the churches were being vexed. There is no mention of prayer when James was killed. It may be, they thought this crisis would pass. Surely God would intervene on their behalf.

This sounds akin to the mentality of our day. No fasting. No praying. No humbling ourselves. We're just waiting for God to intervene. This is not the way God works. God works according to His word. His word says, *"If my people, which are called by my name, shall humble themselves, and pray, and seek my face, and turn from their wicked ways: then will I hear from Heaven, and will forgive their sin, and will heal their land."*

Someone has to pray. Someone has to humble themselves. Someone has to turn from sin before help can be expected from God. This may not fit with the religious thought patterns of today, but it certainly fits the word of God.

This generation has watched as great evangelists have folded their tents and became administrators. We have stood by as gospel singers have become entertainers. Pastors have turned more to public relations and less to preaching.

A list of names could be compiled of men and women who have fallen into all manner of sins such as pornography, adultery, etc.

Has anyone called a prayer meeting? Has anyone humbled themselves? Has the church repented, and turned from sin and the evil of the world, or have we continued going in the same direction? This crisis will continue until the church stops it. There will be other failures, backslidings, scandals, etc.

When Herod apprehended Peter, intending to kill him after Easter, the church decided it was time to stop him. This was the proverbial straw that broke the camel's back. Someone called a prayer meeting.

"Prayer was made without ceasing of the church unto God for him." Without ceasing tells me that they were intending to pray through. They would pray until something happened. This was not a little Wednesday night, thirty minute, powder puff, prayer service. They meant business.

Prayer meetings of this sort move God to action. Divine intervention can be expected when the people of God pray in this fashion. The crisis will pass when praying like this becomes the order of the day.

The night before Peter was to be killed in the morning, the church was praying on Earth, and in Heaven God was hearing those prayers. Somewhere between Heaven and earth the angel of the Lord was on his way to bring an answer to those prayers, and to set the Apostle Peter free. This remedy will yet work today.

- We will never sing our way out of trouble.
- We will never promote our way out of trouble.
- We will never programize our way out of trouble.
- Preaching alone will not deliver us from our trouble.

When the church comes out of the crisis it is in, it will be prayer that gets the job done.

God has heard. An angel has come to the prison to set this man of God free. Great miracles are about to happen. God has arisen, and His power is at work.

Even though God has taken charge of the situation through an answer to prayer, there is still something the church must do to complete this miracle.

How many incomplete miracles has the church experienced? In this hour, we do not need just a touch, we need complete deliverance. We do not need a series of meetings that can almost be called a revival, we need a Holy Ghost explosion.

The angel of the Lord caused the keepers of the prison to fall into a deep sleep. The chains with which Peter was bound fell off. He was then instructed by the angel to dress and bind on his sandals.

So here he stands, fully dressed, and loosed from the chains, but he still faces four locked doors or gates that must be opened before this miracle will be complete.

It's great to have the guards asleep, be free of chains, and standing dressed with sandals on, but the prison doors are still shut and locked. Someone or something must open these doors. For Peter to come out of jail, two cell doors had to be opened for the scripture said, "When they were passed the first and second ward." Then there was the "iron gate that leadeth unto the city." This makes a total of three doors or gates so far that had to be opened. When we add to this the door to Mary's house where the prayer meeting was taking place, we see a total of four doors or gates that will have to be opened for this miracle to be complete.

Who or what power will unlock and open these four doors? Before we answer this question, we should determine who or what power locked each door.

We cannot know the name of the individual who actually turned the key, but we know that the prison cell doors, and the iron gate of the city were locked by the authority of the government. Herod was king. He ruled the jailors and city officials so we could say Herod locked these doors. Herod was an instrument in the hands of Satan, doing his bidding, so we would be right in saying that the ultimate power that closed these doors and locked them to bind the apostle, was the power of Satan.

So Satan locked the first three but who locked the forth door? Since the church was having a prayer meeting in the house, though we don't know the name of the individual man or woman who put the bolt in place, we can say truthfully that the church locked the fourth door.

Now that we know who locked each door, we can answer the question as to who will unlock each door. The first three being locked by the power of Satan, will be unlocked by the power of God. No permission will be needed to accomplish this. Christ never asks permission of Satan to do anything. He just dominates him.

The church need not worry about the devil or the things that he does. When the church prays through and touches God, God will take care of Satan.

What a miracle! The cell doors to the first and second ward open automatically for Peter and the angel. The iron gate of the city opens of its own accord. The apostle never had to touch either one of these.

We hear much talk today about what the devil has done. We worry about the power of Satan. Let the church pray through, get right with God and Satan will have to flee.

After having watched with wonder and holy awe the supernatural way in which the power of God unlocked and opened these doors, it must have been a surprise when Peter came to the place of the prayer meeting and found the door locked tight. The prison doors were no problem. The city gate was not a problem. Never did he so much as lay a finger on either one of these, but lo and behold, the church door is locked. The man of God must stand there and knock hoping someone will hear him and let him in.

It seems that it is easier to get out of Satan's prison than it is to get into the church. What is the difference? If the Holy Ghost would open the first three then why did He refuse to open the fourth one? The Holy Ghost will open the doors that Satan locks in the face of the church, but the doors that the church has locked in the face of God must be opened by the church.

The scripture indicates—by saying, "But Peter continued knocking"—that it took longer to get into the prayer meeting than it did to get out of jail. While the answer to their prayers was standing on the doorsteps, they were trying to determine whether or not a young girl had gone insane because she told them the very thing they were praying for was at the door.

To completely come out of this crisis, the church must open the doors of our hearts and churches to God by removing the things that are keeping Christ and His blessings out of our midst. He will not open the doors the church has locked.

The hardest part of this entire miracle was getting the church to accept what had been done for them.

At the tomb of Lazarus, it was more difficult for Christ to persuade Mary and Martha to remove the stone from the entrance to the tomb than it was to say "Lazarus come forth."

When Jesus said, "Behold, I stand at the door and knock: if any man hear my voice, and open the door, I will come in to him, and sup with him, and he with me." He was not standing at the door of a honky tonk, or a road house somewhere. He was speaking to the church.

Pride, greed, selfishness, flesh, haughty spirits, etc. have shut Christ out of too many churches.

Humility, righteousness, holiness, sanctification, and self-denial will unlock that door allowing the spirit of God to once again fill our churches.

When this happens, the crisis will be over. The church will be restored to its rightful place. Heaven will once again visit earth as the Son of man walks again in the midst of the Candlesticks.

The shout of joy will be heard again in the land. It's time to pray. It's time to repent. It's time to recover and see the church healed.

A generation of young people sit on our church pews who have never witnessed the power of God in action. What a shame. Will we allow them to go through a form of godliness that denies the power of God? Will we lose a generation to hell from our church pews?

Satan is doing some of his greatest work inside the church today. Jesus told the church at Pergamos in the second book of Revelation, "I know where Satan's seat is."

Satan—I am convinced—is more comfortable in a lot of churches than the spirit of God is. Fleshly entertainment is applauded while the works of the spirit are branded as heresy.

We cannot sit around and say that it is yet four months until the harvest. We must lift up our eyes and look on the fields of souls that are ready for harvest.

It is time to be admonished by the words of Christ, "Work while it is day: the night cometh, when no man can." Whatever we plan to do, we must do it quickly.

HELP US LORD. WE NEED A REVIVAL. AMEN.

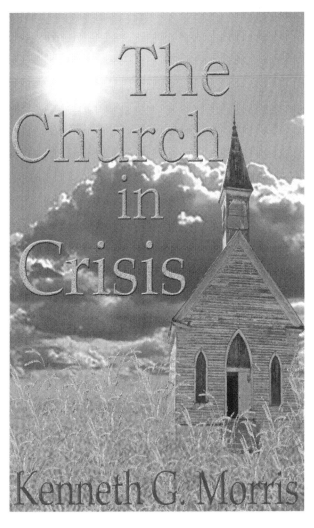

To order additional copies of this book, or to purchase
other books by this author visit
www.empoweredpublicationsinc.com
or ask for them by name at your local bookstore.